Blacks

Bridglal Pachai

NIMBUS
PUBLISHING LTD

Nimbus Publishing Limited
PO Box 9301, Station A
Halifax, NS B3K 5N5
(902) 455-4286

Edited by Lois Kernaghan
Cover photo: Collection of Black Cultural Centre
Printed and bound in Canada

Canadian Cataloguing in Publication Data
Pachai, Bridglal.
Blacks
(Peoples of the Maritimes)
Originally published: Tantallon, N.S.: Four East Publications, 1987.
Includes bibliographical refernces.
ISBN 1-55109-187-9-X
1. Blacks — Maritime Provinces — History.
I. Title   II. Series

FC2050.B6P33 1996   971.5'00496   C96-950114-5
F1035.8.P33 1996

The peoples of the Maritimes comprise in excess of seventy distinct and identifiable ethnic-cultural groups. Yet, only a few of these have their place in our history and our society well known and documented. The Peoples of the Maritimes series is an attempt to redress that imbalance by providing a well researched, but readable collection of monographs for both the general and student reader.

The demographic face of Canada as a whole is changing rapidly as a result of national realities connected with the country's declining birth rate and the need for more immigrants to enhance economic growth. In this context, education and information are crucial for the promotion of harmonious social change.

The Maritimes has rich diversity in its population, ranging all the way from the first nations and the pre-Confederation settlers to the later nation builders from all parts of the globe—more recently from Third World countries in increasing numbers. The literature on the Maritimes must keep pace with these changing times and challenges.

The Maritimes Peoples Project gratefully acknowledges the funding assistance provided for the development of this book by the Minister responsible for Multiculturalism, Government of Canada.

Bridglal Pachai, C.M., Ph.D.
General Editor

Much has happened since an earlier version of this book was published in 1987. Events have taken place with such rapidity that it is clear that another edition may yet be necessary before the end of the present century. This is a good sign. Canadian society is evolving in response to the domestic and international scene.

I am grateful to the following persons for assistance in the form of material supplied or advice received as to source material and contact persons:

John N. Grant (Nova Scotia Teachers College, Truro);

Harry Baglole (Institute of Island Studies, University of Prince Edward Island);

Jim Hornby (Extension Department, University of Prince Edward Island); now lawyer

Donald P. Lemon (New Brunswick Museum);

Nancy McBeath (Public Archives of Prince Edward Island);

Sheila Loatman (Prude Inc., Saint John, New Brunswick);

Elenry Bishop (Black Cultural Centre for Nova Scotia);

Teala Cain, (Prude Inc., Saint John, New Brunswick);

David Peters, (Prude Inc., Saint John, New Brunswick);

Clifford Skinner, Saint John, New Brunswick.

Bridglal Pachai
Halifax, February, 1993

TABLE OF
Contents

CHAPTER 1.
Whence They Came: The Homeland and the Departure

I. Origins

The black presence in the Maritimes goes back to at least the early years of the seventeenth century. In the written records, mention is made of one Mathieu da Costa who came to Port Royal in 1604-1606 in the service of a French colonizing expedition. Da Costa, whose name can be traced to his former status as a slave of the Portuguese, was one of the many Blacks pressed into the service of European colonizers and adventurers from the late fifteenth century onwards. Mathieu Da Costa was one of four men listed as having died of scurvy in the winter of 1606-1607. After Da Costa, mention is made of La Liberté, "le neigre"*, at Cape Sable Island in 1686. La Liberté was possibly an escaped slave from an English colony. Ten years later, in 1696, an English soldier returning from an expedition against the French and their Indian allies in northern Acadia, (later New Brunswick) brought with him a black man. Thus the black presence in what is today New Brunswick can be traced to at least 1696.

In 1739, the French governor of Louisbourg was reported to be in possession of a Black from the island of Martinique. Twenty-seven years later, in 1767, the British lieutenant-governor of Nova Scotia submitted a return for Blacks in the colony, noting that they numbered 104 out of a total population of 13,374. Fifty-four of them were resident in Halifax, two in Canso, seven in Cape Breton Island, six at Annapolis Royal, one at Maugerville (on the Saint John River) and the rest were scattered in different townships.

---

* Historically—and indeed, until the 1960s—the black people have always been referred to as "Negroes" or "coloured", terms now regarded as derogatory. The designation, "Blacks", is used throughout this book. It is recognized that terms such as "Afro-Canadian" and "African-Canadian" are also in use in the 1990s.

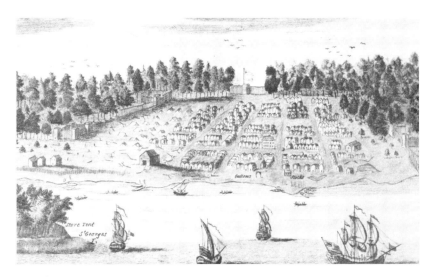

Halifax in 1750.

In a recent publication on Prince Edward Island[*], we are told that "No evidence has been found to indicate that slaves lived on the Island during the French period [i.e. from 1719 - 1763], although in the Ile Saint-Jean census of 1752 several people are listed as "*domestique*".

These returns show that Blacks have lived permanently in most of the Maritimes for some three hundred years. This fact alone qualifies them for inclusion among the first four charter peoples in this region, alongside the Aboriginals, French and English. The returns also emphasize that among the first Blacks in the Maritimes, there were both free persons and slaves.

Free Blacks subsequently entered the Maritimes as part of the Loyalist immigration of 1782-84; as the Maroons from Jamaica, in 1796; as the Black Refugees, during and immediately after the War of 1812; as part of the nineteenth-century immigration from the United States; and as part of the twentieth-century immigration, mainly from the Caribbean, the United States and Africa.

The tradition of Blacks entering the Maritimes as slaves dates

---

[*] Jim Hornby, *Black Islanders. Prince Edward Island's Historical Black Community*, p.1.

8 **Blacks**

predominantly from 1760, when slavery was accorded legal recognition in British North America during the Seven Years' War, to 1834, when slavery was abolished throughout the British Empire. The institution was not popular in the Maritimes after about 1800, however, and had virtually ceased before emancipation day, August 1, 1834.

When one considers the origins of Blacks in the Maritimes— whether free persons, slaves, Black Loyalists, Maroons, Black Refugees, the later immigrants from near and far, or the descendants of all of these streams—one must turn to the continent of Africa, the ancestral home of the founders of the black population in the Maritimes. It was from West Africa that men, women and children were taken in slavery and removed to Europe, the Americas and the Caribbean.

During the four hundred years between 1450 and 1850, many millions were transported across the seas. The actual numbers are difficult to determine; previously estimates went as high as 50 million but, more recently and after years of careful research, the numbers have been placed at between 11 and 15 million. Whatever figure one settles for, the count is high. It becomes even higher when one adds to this number those who died while being transported. Today, more than one hundred million persons of African descent, whose forbears were once forcibly and cruelly removed from their homeland, live in different parts of the world, including the Maritimes.

II. Geography and Society

Africa is the second largest continent in the world. It extends for almost 6400 km (4000 mi.) from north to south, covering some 30.3 million square km (11.17 million sq. mi.) of land, with large lakes, rivers and mountains. Today, some eight hundred different languages have been identified. The continent is made up at present of 52 countries. Africa has suffered much in the past, and continues to suffer from desert conditions, drought, famine, diseases and poor transportation. It has suffered, too, from the ravages of the slave trade and from exploitation both during and after the period of European colonization.

The Africa from which the early slaves were removed was a complex and highly-developed society. The human history of the continent goes back nearly three million years. Anthropologists are in agreement that Africa has made an important contribution to the evolution of the human species; to the development of stone and iron tools and technology; to the development of agriculture; and to the rise of the early kingdoms and civilization associated with such places as Egypt, Ghana, Mali, Songhai and Zimbabwe. Independent and viable political and religious systems which regulated the life of the people from birth to death existed in Africa long before foreigners came to that continent. Social customs developed roles for everyone, while the division of labour created responsibilities for men, women and children; societies decided by consensus what codes of conduct should be practiced. Traditional systems of justice laid down judicial procedures and the elders and counsellors were well versed in their duties. Land was the common wealth and inheritance of the people, and a well-defined system of land use and occupation existed.

It was, then the descendants of this complex and highly-developed continent in social and cultural terms who were destined at different times to comprise the black population of the Maritimes.

CHAPTER 2.
Settling In: Adjusting to the New Land

I. Early Beginnings

Slavery was practised in the Maritimes even before 1760. In September 1751, an advertisement appeared in the Boston *Evening Post*, offering ten Blacks from Halifax for sale; they were described as caulkers, carpenters, sail-makers and rope-makers. The sale of slaves by public auction was common in Nova Scotia in the eighteenth century. There is evidence also of the existence of slavery in New Brunswick from 1767 and in Prince Edward Island since the 1780s.

II. The Loyalist Period

The first sizeable influx of Blacks to the Maritimes occurred as a result of the Loyalist immigration during the American War of Independence, 1775-1783. More than three thousand free Blacks or former slaves who were on the side of the British during the war earned the right to passage to Nova Scotia. As a result, 1336 men, 914 women and 750 children came to this province in 1783, while 225 went to Europe, Quebec or the West Indies. Smaller numbers arrived in 1776 and 1782, Most of these immigrants had been born in Africa, or were only a generation removed from the painful slve journey to America. The majority were transported in 1783 in 81 vessels departing from New York. Of the 2775 who came to Nova Scotia, 1423 sailed under the category of "Black Companies", which recognized their previous status as fighting men. Some came as hired, indentured or apprenticed persons, attached to white Loyalist civilians or disbanded officers. A few arrived without any such connection and were designated as having come "on his or her own Bottom".

In addition to the 2775 free persons, 1232 came as slaves to white Loyalist owners; they formed the largest single addition made to the black slave population of the Maritimes. These slaves were distributed as follows: Dartmouth, 41; Country Harbour, 41; Chedabucto, 61; St. John's Island (later Prince Edward Island), 26; Antigonish, 18; Cumberland, 21; Partridge Island (later Parrsboro), 69; Cornwallis and Horton, 38; Newport and Kennetcook, 22; Windsor, 21; Annapolis Royal, 230; Digby, 152; St. Mary's Bay, 13; River St. John (later New Brunswick), 441. The number not accounted for must have been directed to Shelburne or Cape Breton, neither of which was listed in the distribution; both places were known to have had slaves.

To these initial numbers of 2775 free Blacks and 1232 enslaved Blacks who arrived in 1783, must be added others who soon followed. The largest concentration of both free Blacks and slaves was in Port Roseway, soon renamed Shelburne, a city carved out of the wilderness for white Loyalists, and in its satellite, Birchtown, a black settlement with a population of 2700 in 1784—perhaps one of the largest urban concentrations of Blacks outside Africa at the time.

In that same year, the province of New Brunswick was created. In addition to the 441 slaves already there, 433 free Blacks arrived in 1784, making a total black population of 874. In the third region of the Maritimes, St. John's Island (which became Prince Edward Island in 1799), 26 black slaves were accounted for in 1783 to which, a year later, was added a further 16 black servants and a small number of slaves brought by their masters from the United States.

Thus, in 1784, there were in the Maritimes some 3500 free Blacks and some 1200 other Blacks referred to as "servants" or "slaves". These terms were used interchangeably and the distinction between them was often confusing. Slave owners were inclined to hide the real situation as moral indignation against slavery increased. In some cases, free Blacks bound over their children, as did adult white people in strained circumstances. The distinctions, however, were less important than the immediate problems and challenges which faced these 4000 new arrivals in a land where climate, soil, bureaucratic indifference and racial discrimination combined to make their entry both inhospitable and unrewarding.

All Loyalists, whether white or black, were promised free grants of land in the new country. The problems lay in the amount and quality of the acreage available; in the system adopted for the allocation and distribution of land; in the administrative incompetence, made worse by the shortage of financial and human resources in the civil service; and in the sheer numbers of people—estimated at nearly 30,000—clamour-

NEW-YORK, 2*1*t *april* 1783.

THIS is to certify to whomfoever it may concern, that the Bearer hereof *Cato Hanw*...*day* a Negro, reforted to the Britifh Lines, in confequence of the Proclamations of Sir William Howe, and Sir Henry Clinton, late Commanders in Chief in America ; and that the faid Negro has hereby his Excellency Sir Guy Carleton's Permillion to go to Nova-Scotia, or wherever elfe *He* may think proper.

Documents like this one were issued by the British to loyal blacks at war's end, and served as a passport to Canada.

Black Cultural Centre

ing for attention. In such a situation, Blacks stood to lose, and to lose the most. In the social and economic scale, they stood at the end of the line.

In 1783, there were some 14 million hectares (26 million acres) of land in Nova Scotia as it was constituted at that time. Half this amount had already been taken up by earlier allocations to immigrants from Europe and the New England colonies. The principle adopted in making the new distribution was that those who had lost most in the war were to be served first. The size of the grants in such cases was to be in keeping with the estates they had left behind in the United States. Less prosperous refugees were to receive one hundred acres for the head of the family, plus 50 acres for each family member, including slaves attached to the household. Disbanded military men received grants according to rank, ranging from 1000 acres for a field officer to one hundred acres for a private soldier, plus allowances for family members.

None of these provisions was helpful to the Blacks, who were placed at the end of a long bureaucratic line. Two-and-a-half years later, in 1786, almost all the white Loyalists in Shelburne County had received their grants. The first Blacks had to wait till 1787, when grants were made to 184 of 649 black men in Birchtown. The average allocation for the whites was 74 acres; for the Blacks it was 34. Some Blacks were granted small town lots and with their savings purchased farms in Birchtown; some had even purchased their town lots. What this meant was that only one-third of the inhabitants in the largest settlement of Loyalist Blacks in Nova Scotia received any government land at all. For this they had to wait four-and-a-half years.

What happened in Birchtown found echoes in other parts of the province. A significant number of former members of the Black Pioneers, the only all-black regiment raised by Great Britain during the Revolution, had settled in Digby and nearby Brindley Town. Difficulties were encountered in settling the veterans, and four petitions were submitted drawing attention to the delays in land grants. These petitions were master-minded by Thomas Peters and Murphy Still, former sargeants of the Black Pioneers, and by Joseph Leonard. The end result of these efforts, which extended over a period of six years from 1783 to 1789, was that 76 one-acre town lots in Brindley Town were the only lots granted to the second largest Black Loyalist concentration in Nova Scotia.

A third area of black concentration was in Little Tracadie, near Guysborough. There the leader, Thomas Brownspriggs, successfully petitioned for land grants for 74 black families who were still unattended to as late as September 1787, when 40-acre grants were at last issued to each family.

In a fourth area of black concentration, Preston, near Dartmouth, white families and 29 black families were originally settled in 1783. When the grants were issued a year later, the average size of the allocations to whites was 204 acres, and that of Blacks was 50 acres. By then, many more of both races had moved into the area, but out of a possible one hundred black families, only ten members of the black community in Preston were the recipients of the 50-acre grants in 1784.

The unfortunate plight of the black residents of both Digby and

Preston, where the majority remained landless, was due not to any shortage of land, but instead to problems relating to the cost of layout out the individual lots. Government funds were withdrawn before the surveying project would be completed throughout the province, and individual Blacks were too poor to pay the costs themselves.

Their situation emphasized the general government mismanagement evident throughout the province during the settling of the loyalists. In this instance, there was little point in promising free acreage for previous services rendered, if the poor Blacks in a strange land were to pay the surveyors' fees themselves.

There were similar problems in New Brunswick, where 433 free Blacks were granted town lots in Saint John. These lots proved to be too small for a living. The government advised these Blacks who wished to become farmers to form themselves into companies and to apply for vacant lands to be surveyed, cut up into 50-acre lots, and then issued. Three companies were formed, laying claim to 121 lots in total. Very few of these were ever taken up, however, since most of the Blacks were not keen on farming and preferred wage labour within white communities. It was not until 1812 that the first successful black settlement was set up in New Brunswick, at a place called Otnabog, through the initiative of freed slaves and free Blacks descended from the Black Loyalists.

Prince Edward Island attempted to attract slaves without much success. Its first governor, Walter Patterson, reported to London in 1774 that the Island had 1215 whites, but no Blacks. In 1781 he passed an Act providing that baptism of slaves would not free them from bondage. This did little to attract slave holders to the Island. Ten years later, Patterson's successor introduced an Act permitting immigrants from the United States to import "Negroes" with their other property with the stipulation that they could only be sold after a year. Thus sale of slaves became legal in Prince Edward Island. "Although the number of slaves on the Island will never be known, it is now obvious that from the 1780s until after 1800, the local elite—both Loyalist and others—was largely a slave-owning group."*

The disappointing experience of the Black Loyalists in their expectation of receiving grants of sufficient land to set them on their way to becoming worthy citizens in the promised land destroyed their

* Jim Hornby, *Black Islanders*, p. 10

morale. Worse followed, in the form of exploitation of cheap labour, racial riots in which the properties of Blacks were destroyed in Birchtown and Shelburne, and general shortages of food and clothing. In his autobiography, the Methodist preacher, Boston King, who lived in Birchtown and worked as a carpenter, described the harsh winter of 1789, which was compounded by famine:

> Many of the poor people were compelled to sell their best gowns for five pounds of flour, in order to support life. When they had parted with all their clothes, even to their blankets, several of them fell down dead in the streets through hunger. Some killed and eat [sic] their dogs and cats; and poverty and distress prevailed on every side.*

The racial riots which erupted in Shelburne in 1784 and spread to Birchtown were documented in a diary kept by the town's surveyor, Benjamin Marston. He noted that the disturbances resulted from complaints by the white Loyalists that the free Blacks were providing cheap labour. Economic issues were thus beginning to create serious divisions in colonial society. Already other cleavages were becoming obvious: free Blacks, even those in possession of land, were not allowed to vote, but were nevertheless subject to taxation. Clearly, as a land of refuge and hope, the Maritimes of the eighteenth century offered little to the poor, less to the free Blacks, and least of all to the slaves.

It is true that the number of slaves in the Maritimes, and indeed in all of Canada, was small compared to the United States. However, during the Loyalist period, fully one-quarter of the black population in the Maritimes were enslaved. This placed them at the bottom of the disadvantaged pack. Due to the climate and lack of any major crop such as cotton, however, there was little economic need for slave labour in the Maritimes, and the institution was not popular locally. In general, slaves received fair treatment because of their importance in the domestic household and because of the skills they possessed as craftspersons.

For all that, slaves were still slaves. As chattel, they were liable to be sold at any time without regard for family ties. Where mothers were separated from children and husbands separated from wives, where human beings were sold in public auction alongside cattle and household goods, it mattered little what kind of "humane" treatment was accorded them by their owners.

* Cited in Ellen Gibson Wilson, *The Loyal Blacks* (New York and Toronto, 1976), p. 91

The law courts, however, led by strong personalities like Ward Chipman, one-time attorney-general and chief justice of New Brunswick, and chief justices Andrew Strange and Sampson Salter Blowers of Nova Scotia, came to the defence of slaves in the Maritimes in the early years of the nineteenth century. When slavery was finally abolished in the British Empire in 1834, it had long ceased to be of any relevance in the Maritimes, for there were no more slaves to be freed.

Without the promised land, without gainful employment, without the right to vote or the right to trial by jury, and without the freedom to attend the same churches and schools as the white population, the Black Loyalists had no choice but to turn to one another to work out their own strategy for survival. In New Brunswick, Governor Thomas Carleton summed up the "extent of his government's responsibility towards these displaced patriotic persons: to provide for their personal protection and for freedom from slavery; the rest was up to the Blacks themselves."

Throughout the Maritimes, they took up the challenge and established their own churches and schools. The organization of their religious life was particularly important. Separate Anglican and Methodist congregations were set up with the aid of white supporters notably at Birchtown, Brindley Town and Little Tracadie; these congregations were led by, respectively, Isaac Limerick, Joseph Leonard and Thomas Brownspriggs. The Anglican connection produced such black leaders as William Furmage, Cato Perkins and William Ash. The notable black Methodist leaders were the blind and lame Moses Wilkinson, Boston King and John Ball.

A special place belongs to the Baptist Church in the history of the Maritime Blacks. Alone among all the denominations, the black Baptist chapels were the only ones founded and maintained without the support of any white agent or agency. The name of David George is pre-eminent among the early black Baptist leaders. He had been one of the first embers, and later the pastor, of North America's first black church, at Sillver Bluff in South Carolina. He came to Shelburne in 1784, had his full share of problems in that strife-ridden community, visited Saint John and Fredericton on a highly-successful preaching tour, and ended by undertaking a grand tour through Nova Scotia, to such places as Horton, Preston, Halifax, Digby and Liverpool. He founded chapels and appointed elders in all these communities, and enraged the white population by personally baptizing those whites who wished to become members of his congregation, an action which was deemed highly

An outdoor baptism, traditional in the black Baptist Church.

improper at that time. He is today remembered and honoured as the founder of the black Baptist church in the Maritimes. A new book on David George was published in 1992.*

The separate black schools which were established at the same time as the separate black churches owed their origin to the initiatives of independent white bodies, such as the Anglican Society for the Propagation of the Gospel. The early church leaders were also the first school teachers, and included such individuals as Colonel Stephen Blucke and Mrs. Catherine Abernathy in Nova Scotia.

An interesting aspect of the history of Blacks in the Maritimes which has still to be researched and presented in detail is the story from the point of view of the principal subjects themselves. Among the few personal accounts that have been used are those by David George (*Baptist Annual Register*, Vol. I, 1790-1793, pp. 473-484) and Boston King (*The Methodist Magazine*, Vol. XXI, 1798), both of whom came to Nova Scotia with the Black Loyalists in 1782-83 and emigrated to sierra Leone in 1792.

A pioneering study by Jim Hornby gives an account of slavery on

* Grant Gordon, From Slavery to Freedom. *The Life of David George, Pioneer Baptist Minister.*

Prince Edward Island from the slaves' point of view. Future researchers would make a valuable contribution with similar studies in New Brunswick and Nova Scotia. Using court records, Hornby's study gives the experiences of Island Blacks named Jupiter Wise, Thomas Williams, William Bellinger, Susannah Schurman, Freelove Haszard Allen, David Sheppard, Dimbo Suckles, James MacDonald, and John and Amelia Byers and other members of the Byers family* Their experiences throw light on the severe exploitation by the existing social and bureaucratic systems and provide a basis for measuring changes that have taken place as well as improvements that have still to be made.

III. Exodus to Sierra Leone

The general disenchantment of the Black Loyalists with their new life in the Maritimes soon found expression. One of the most vocal and influential of the group was Thomas Peters, who led many of his fellow Blacks in an exodus from Nova Scotia to Sierra Leone in 1792. Peters escaped from slavery in North Carolina in 1776, became a sergeant in the Black Pioneers, immigrated to Nova Scotia in 1784, and quickly assumed leadership of the Blacks in the Digby area. When his efforts to obtain land for himself and his people there went unanswered, he made a similar effort, also unsuccessful, in New Brunswick.

He then went directly to London, where he presented a petition outlining his difficulties to the British government. While there, Peters also outlined the other dissatisfactions felt by his people over the lack of recognition and equality shown to them by the colonial administration. In addition, he met with and was impressed by, representatives of the Sierra Leone Company, who were attempting to attract black settlers to their colony in Africa.

As a result of all this, both the governors of Nova Scotia and New Brunswick were subsequently ordered to conduct an investigation into the complaints of the Blacks concerning land allocation. They were also required to ascertain how many of the Blacks were willing to emigrate to Sierra Leone, or to enlist for British military service in the West Indies.

Lieutenant John Clarkson, an agent of the Sierra Leone Company and brother of the abolitionist Thomas Clarkson, arrived in Nova Scotia in October 1791. Three months later, on 15 January 1792, some 1196

---

*   Jim Hornby, *Black Islanders*, "Lives Under Slavery", 1784-1832, pp. 15-44.

Sierra Leone, the final destination for many Black Loyalists.

members of the black population of the Maritimes left for Sierra Leone, among them the prominent leaders of that time: Thomas Peters, David George, Moses Wilkinson, John Ball, Cato Perkins, Joseph Leonard, Boston King, Hector Peters and Adam and Catherine Abernathy.

They and their followers left because of a combination of three expectations that had remained largely unfulfilled: free grants of sufficient land, full independence and security of life and property. Even then, before their departure, they had to prove that they were free in status, free of debt and of good character; furthermore , their statements had to be certified by those of their countrymen who were least willing to see them go because of their proven skills, cheap labour and market produce. In the end it was the position taken by black leaders such as Thomas Peters and David George that tipped the scale in favour of the exodus: they had visions of unfettered freedom in their ancestral home.

The emigration to Sierra Leone removed about half the black population of the Maritimes. Of those who remained, few did so by chance; slaves, indentured labourers, sharecroppers, the aged and infirm, the unskilled and those in debt had little alternative. Clearly, the cream of the crop left for Africa in 1792. Even with the numbers cut down by half, the situation concerning land grants remained unchanged. Petitions from landless Blacks in the Maritimes continued to appear and went unanswered, while the majority of the remaining Black Loyalists tended to migrate to the larger centres of Halifax, Fredericton and Saint John in search of paid employment. Bereft of their leaders, the black churches and schools closed down. The black settlements were shattered: Preston was deserted; only a quarter of the black population of Brindley Town and half of the population of Birchtown remained; Little Tracadie was the only black settlement unaffected by the exodus of 1792.

IV. The Maroons

In the midst of this painful period of adjustment, some 550 Jamaican Maroons landed in Halifax in July 1796. These were martial people with a long tradition of resistance to European rule in Jamaica and the adjacent islands. Though recently defeated and expelled, they were received in Nova Scotia with greater awe and consideration than was ever bestowed on any black group previously in the Maritimes. They were put to work in building the fortification at the Citadel in Halifax, accommodated in nearby rented premises, and kept under surveillance so as to ensure they did not disturb the peace. However, the cold climate of Nova Scotia, their isolation from familiar surroundings, and the disruption of their lifestyles combined to arouse murmurings of discontent. The government was much relieved to see them depart for Sierra Leone in August 1800.

While the majority of the Maroon population left for Sierra Leone in 1800, a few remained behind. This residue grew over the years into at least one large family whose roots go back to the Maroon period in Nova Scotia. This is the Colley family descended from Sarah Colley, the Maroon mistress of Governor Sir John Wentworth. Their son, George Wentworth Colley, was born on August 16, 1804 and died on November 2, 1893. George Wentworth Colley inherited the governor's summer house located on what is today known as Colley's farm on Upper Governor's Road in East Preston. A hundred years after his death, members of the Colley family are still contesting what they allege to be alienation of their property. The Maroon legacy lives on in Nova Scotia.

The latest study on the Maroons by Dr. John Grant of the Nova Scotia Teachers College bears a fascinating title: "From Trelawny Town to Granville Town - The Maroon Town Interlude: the Maroons in Nova Scotia".

Maroons meeting with British officers.

V. The Refugee Blacks

Thirteen years later, the vanguard of the most important group of Blacks to settle in the Maritimes made its appearance. Over a three-year period from 1813 to 1816, some 2000 Black Refugees fled north from the United States in the same circumstances as had their predecessors, the Black Loyalists. These Black Refugees were escaped slaves who had thrown in their lot with the British during the War of 1812; they now came as free Blacks to take up residence on British soil in the Maritimes.

Early in 1815, between four and five hundred of these new arrivals were sent to New Brunswick, where they founded the settlement of Loch Lomond as a result of 50-acre land grants made to most of them. By end of December 1816, the figure for Nova Scotia was 1619 new arrivals, made up as follows: 924 at Preston, 504 at Hammonds Plains, 76 at Refugee Hill and 115 in Halifax.

They could not have arrived at a worse time in Nova Scotia: in 1816 the winter was particularly harsh and a poor harvest resulted in severe food shortages; in 1817 mice and rodents ravaged the crops. Added to these natural disasters, the buoyant economy of the previous few years during the War of 1812 took a downward turn and the number of unemployed increased sharply. Food, clothing and shelter were badly needed among the Refugee Blacks, especially for the old and infirm, most of whom were admitted to the Poor House in Halifax, on a daily average of 55 persons.

The plight of the poor Blacks soon received the attention of the House of Assembly, which called for statistical information to determine the extent of the problem, since conflicting reports had been received regarding the ability and industry of the refugees. While the assembly was prepared to help the sick and needy on this occasion, it was reminded by certain of its members in 1815

> that the proportion of Africans already in this country is productive of many inconveniences; and that the introduction of more must tend to the discouragement of white labourers and servants, as well as to the establishment of a separate and marked class of people, unfitted by nature to this climate, or to an association with the rest of His Majesty's Colonists.*

The observations made in the House of Assembly back in 1815, outlining the ways in which the unsympathetic white population of that time viewed the black minority in Nova Scotia, are worth recalling today. Most if not all of the comments still hold true: Blacks were an inconvenience; their numbers should be kept down in the interest of the

---

* C. Bruce Fergusson, *A Documentary Study of the Establishment of the Negroes in Nova Scotia Between the War of 1812 and the Winning of Responsible Government* (Public Archives of Nova Scotia, Bulletin No. 8, 1948), p. 21

white working class; Blacks were visibly different, which contributed to the need for segregation; Black's were unsuited to Canada's climate (1909 a Black named Matthew Henson became co-discoverer of the North Pole); and Blacks could not be integrated. Consequently, much of the story of the black presence in the Maritimes since 1815 can be stated under such general themes as the period of neglect (1815-c. 1960); the period of discovery (c.1960-c.1980); and the period of co-existence (c.1980 onwards). Only the future can be expected to provide the period of partnership among equals, which is where all the earlier efforts should end, in eventual realization of the status of equal partners in the mainstream of Canadian society.

CHAPTER 3

History in the Maritimes

I. Distribution of Blacks in the Maritimes

During the whole of the nineteenth century, and up to the late 1970s, Blacks in the Maritimes lived on the periphery of the available occupational positions. Of the estimated population of 10,000 Blacks in the Maritimes at the opening of the present century, over three-quarters lived in Nova Scotia, mainly within a radius of 15-20 miles from the centre of Halifax. In New Brunswick, the Loch Lomond settlement near Saint John turned out to be the main concentration. In addition to the grants made in 1815, some 112 lots of 55 acres each were issued under licenses of occupation, (far inferior to title deeds) from 1837 onwards; yet by 1904 only twenty families remained in the whole settlement. On Prince Edward Island, the black population has always been very small, estimated at 155 in 1881. In the second half of the nineteenth century, most of them lived in what was called the Bog (or West Bog), around upper Rockford Street in Charlottetown. Here, for years, the Old Bog School served the Blacks as well as poor whites in the area. By 1921 the black population of Charlottetown was down to 43.

Three factors have, in the main, contributed to the general poverty suffered by Blacks in the Maritimes; lands granted on the basis of licenses of occupation; racial prejudice and discrimination; and poor education, which has compounded the difficulties experienced in any effort to achieve upward mobility in the job market.

II. Problems Associated with Land Ownership

The early difficulties experienced by the Black Loyalists in the allocation of land have already been mentioned. The Black Refugees of 1813-16 and their descendants had similar problems in Nova Scotia and New Brunswick. Full land grants, including title deeds, were withheld, in many cases for more than 30 years. Indeed, as late as 1985, some land titles were still in dispute. A licence of occupation was a poor alternative, since the property and improvements could not be sold or mortgaged to raise funds.

Certain additional problems encountered in the Preston area of Halifax County were not uncommon in other places. There, small lots of 10 acres were situated in swampy areas or on barren, unproductive land. The Commissioner of Crown Lands advised in 1841 that, because of the harsh climate, at least one hundred acres would be required for each family to grow food crops and to obtain wood for fuel. By then many things had already happened: in 1827 the British government abolished the system of free land grants. Instead, and to cut down on relief costs incurred to maintain the poverty stricken Blacks, the government authorized in 1839 the grant of unoccupied Crown lands by licences of occupation. This scheme was unpopular because it would have splintered the community by scattering it elsewhere in small pockets. Eventually an exception was made in the case of Preston and outright free grants were issued in 1841: properties could now be sold and money raised for development. A similar situation developed in the Willow Grove settlement near Saint John, New Brunswick, and land grants with full title were only issued in 1836.

In the Maritimes, and indeed all over Canada, one black settlement deserves special mention—that of Africville, located in the Bedford Basin area of Halifax, today the site of Seaview Park at the foot of the A. Murray MacKay bridge. Seaview Park was opened on June 23, 1985 and aroused nostalgic memories among the black population who saw in this situation another reminder of the unfair treatment meted out to them in the past. The first Africville settlers were Blacks who relocated from Preston and Hammonds Plains between c. 1835 and c. 1845 to take economic advantage of the proximity to the city docks and shipbuilding yards. The settlement developed as a secluded, segregated, neglected part of Halifax. Flanked by Bedford Basin on one side, the railway line on another, and the city dump on the third, Africville grew into a bush area with small farms on which poultry, horses and goats were raised. Fishing was another important occupation.

As industries sprang up in the vicinity and city waste was dumped into the open nearby, conditions in Africville deteriorated. The initial population of some 54 Blacks in 1851 increased to about four hundred in 1964, when the City of Halifax decided to relocate the residents. Here was a community more than one hundred years old with its own church, school and sub-post office. Because it was a segregated black community, however, it had never received proper city health services, roads, water or electricity. It took a decade to uproot the distressed residents. In the end, Africville moved into history as a tragic example of the misery inflicted on Blacks by a policy of neglect through segregation.

Though lesser known, Charlottetown's black district in Prince Edward Island, "The Bog", has a history that reminds one of Africville. Founded by a former slave named Samuel Martin who petitioned for permission to occupy a vacant land in 1813, it was located adjacent to Governor's Pond. The Bog and the Pond were linked by a bridge known locally as "Sam's Bridge", "Samuel Martin's Bridge" and "Black Sam's Bridge".

As in the case of Africville where certain surnames were common—Brown, Thomas, Carvery, Dixon—in the Bog common black surnames were Byers, Sheppard, Mills, Potter, Carpenter, Crosby, DeCourcey and Ryan. While most Africvilleans were members of the Baptist faith, most Bog residents were Roman Catholics.

While the Bog was a racially mixed community, characterized as members of the poor class, Africville was a black community striving to hold its own in a racist society, proud of its fine houses, space, small-scale businesses and strong community spirit.

III. Prejudice, Discrimination and Education

The other causative factors of black poverty—racial prejudice and discrimination—are so closely interlinked that they can be treated together. The root cause of the development of these factors over a period of two hundred years must be traced to the fact that Canada was once a slave society. Consequently, the attitudes and prejudices that became hardened over the years were born out of the circumstances of such a society. Instances of racial discrimination can be drawn from all parts of the Maritimes. A few of the more obvious ones will serve to illustrate the point.

In the 1870s the Halifax City Council excluded Blacks from the common schools. In 1907 a bylaw was passed in St. Croix, in Hants County, Nova Scotia, excluding Blacks from burial in the local cemetery. Separate seating arrangements were standard in theatres throughout the Maritimes, as exemplified in the classic case concerning Mrs. Viola Desmond, who was charged in New Glasgow, Nova Scotia, in

1946 for occupying a downstairs seat, instead of a balcony one set aside for Blacks. Mrs. Desmond spent a night in jail and was later fined $20 and costs. Though the sentence was reversed on appeal, the point was clear that the segregated pews, segregated churches, segregated schools and segregated communities of almost two hundred years ago were still very much in existence in the middle years of the twentieth century.

In New Brunswick, the charter of the city of Saint John, dated April 30, 1785, debarred Blacks from practising any trade within the city limits, except under special licences granted to "good and decent honest persons".

What was "good, decent and honest" was illustrated sadly in an incident which occurred in Charlottetown's West Bog district on August 14, 1878. A sixteen-year-old Black was shot and killed by two whites who were identified by black eye witnesses. What was significant in the trial that followed was that cultures and communities were dragged into the courtroom. The witnesses to the crime were likened by counsel for the defence to "thieves and prostitutes . . . brought up in evil and vice from the time they were children . . . caring nothing for an oath, and thinking of nothing but the fleeting passions of the hour to obtain what they desire". The attorney-general, in an attempt at fairness, objected to the denunciation of an entire community: "Their colour may not be so white as that of some other persons; but if we believe the Scriptures, they all belong to the same great brotherhood as ourselves . . . There are good and bad people in the Bog, as well as anywhere else. The base passions of humanity are not confined to poor people or to black people."* The acquittal that followed was in line with the standards of the time.

Another characteristic of the standards of that earlier time, which has left a negative legacy for the black communities to overcome, was the existence of segregated schools. The wider ramifications of this have been felt in the poor quality of education, in a negative attitude towards learning, and in the stereotype that Blacks are unwilling or unable (or both) to advance through acquiring a sound education. Until very recent times, there have been few highly-qualified black teachers, scientists and professionals in the Maritimes. According to one reliable survey conducted in 1964, the Nova Scotian black community, which then numbered about 10,000, counted only two doctors, two lawyers, six

---

* Greg Marquis, "Murder in the Bog", *The Island Magazine*, No. 14(2), Fall-Winter 1933, pp. 29-32.

Black school children.

ordained ministers, two nurses and about 30 teachers among its ranks.

In Charlottetown, Prince Edward Island, the black population living in The Bog area, was not served by a separate or segregated school. The area was racially mixed. Unlike in Nova Scotia and New Brunswick where a combination of law and practice provided for segregated schools for black children, the Island had racially mixed schools. The Bog School opened in April, 1848 under the auspices of the Anglican Church. What set this school apart was its location in the poorest section of the town. When a new school was erected in 1868, its name was changed to West End School to improve the image that it catered for "Negroes and debased whites". But until it finally closed its doors in 1903, it continued to be known as the Bog School.

The first separate school for black children in Saint John, New Brunswick, opened in 1820. A year earlier, a common school had started in Fredericton for both white and black children, but this open provision lasted for a year only and was replaced by a separate school for Blacks in 1820. These schools ceased to exist after 1838. Other separate schools for Blacks which also lasted for short periods of time were in Loch Lomond, Kingsclear (York County), Elm Hill and Willow Grove. Another school was opened in Saint John in 1840, and, at the turn of the century, two schools for black children existed there. The attendance in all these schools was very small. This must be seen in the light of the prejudices of the time, which did not appear to reward educational achievements. Both opportunities and incentives were lacking; the image of Blacks as servants and labourers was too powerful to be broken.

The first black university graduate in New Brunswick, Arthur Richardson, obtained an honours degree in classics in 1886, while the first black woman, Mary Matilda Winslow, graduated in 1905. Neither could obtain teaching positions in New Brunswick and both worked in segregated black institutions elsewhere before moving off to better prospects in the United States. Richardson taught for a while at the Wilberforce Institute in Chatham, Ontario, while Winslow taught at a school near Halifax. The first black teacher, William Gosman, qualified in 1866 and taught school at the black settlement of Elm Hill before taking the familiar road to the United States.

Though the separate schools of New Brunswick were not created by legislation, *de facto* segregation had the same practical effect as *de jure* segregation. As soon as black faces appeared in numbers beyond one's fingertips, the hostility of white parents and children made life unbearable for black children. The aim was to drive them to separate schools. To say that "black children mixed readily with white [where] the negro population was small", and that "two coloured students enrolled with eighty white children"* at St. Andrews in 1831 is to neutralize the severity of the racial discrimination prevalent throughout the school system.

In Nova Scotia the position was only slightly different. After 1811, communities which were able to contribute financially towards starting a school had their funds matched by an equal amount in the form of provincial grants. Since the black communities were rarely able to raise their share, many such communities went without school. Consequently, special government grants were introduced to support private and segregated schools for black children in Halifax, Preston, Hammonds Plains, Granville, Birchtown, Port Latour, Brindley Town and Liverpool. After 1884, school commissioners had the legal power to set up separate schools as the need arose. Since separate black communities existed as a fact of life, separate schools were a natural result of this pattern.

Legal segregation was finally abolished in 1954, but separate communities lived on and *de facto* segregated schools thus remained. The point must be made that many communities remained without schools at all, some with intermittent schools, and a few with schools but no regular teachers. As late as 1970 the highest grade available in these *de facto* segregated institutions was grade 6. School buses required to

* Robin W. Winks, *the Blacks in Canada* (Montreal, 1971), p. 365

Black women have traditionally found domestic employment.

Black Cultural Centre

take black children to integrated secondary schools did not stop in black settlements. Progress, therefore, has been very slow and uneven.

Poor education and racial discrimination have serious implications for economic progress. Throughout the history of black settlements in the Maritimes, Blacks have occupied the lowest social and economic positions in the vertical mosaic (excluding Canadian Indians in this instance, because of the special status accorded to them). In urban areas black women have worked for more than a century as domestic cleaners, while black males have been employed mainly in the service industry, as freelance gardeners, handymen, heavy cleaners and railway por-ters—even losing out in some of these positions once salary scales and other benefits become more attractive to white applicants.

In rural areas the situation has been worse. Most Blacks have had no farms of their own on which to make a living. In a 1964 study carried out in the three black communities in Guysborough County, Nova Scotia, it was discovered that of the 149 individuals who made up the black labour force, 115 earned less than $1000 annually. Extended to the entire Maritimes, the study concluded that one-half of the rural black wage earners had incomes of less than $2000 annually. The investiga-tion concluded "that a strong case can be made for the position that rural non-farm workers constitute an exploited class."*

* Donald H. Clairmont and Dennis W. Magill, *Nova Scotian Blacks: An Historical and Structural Overview* (Halifax, 1970) p. 67.

A chauffeur.

Black Cultural Centre

Placed in the broader context of Canadian society, black people in the Maritimes, as in the rest of Canada, have all suffered from one form of exploitation or another for more than three hundred years, since the first Blacks arrived on Canadian soil. Over the years they have striven to improve their lot, placing their reliance on God, their chosen leaders, their community organizations, and to a lesser extent, their provincial and regional governing bodies. Beginning with an abiding faith in the tenets of the Christian religion, which has served to unite the people and provide them with inspiration and guidance, the leaders and the organizations have been deeply influenced by Christianity and its teachings. Until recently, advancement and prominence within the church structure has been almost the only means by which Maritime Blacks have been able to achieve distinction and cultural identity.

The treatment accorded to William Hall, V.C., for his distinguished services to the British Empire reflects the treatment accorded to Blacks in general during the period covered by his life. The belated efforts undertaken posthumously in the 1930s and later to honour his memory are similarly symptomatic of a gradual, though at times cosmetic, change of attitude towards Blacks.

CHAPTER 4
Prominent Individuals and Institutions

The black church leaders produced in the eighteenth century should be remembered for their contribution to the history of the Maritimes, even if their stay in the region was all too short. Their pioneering work had many lessons for future generations of Maritimers, both black and non-black. Two of the outstanding personalities chosen by way of examples are David George and Boston King. A secular leader, Thomas Peters, makes up the trio who headed the list of Black Loyalist diaspora to Sierra Leone in 1792.

Mention has already been made of David George. The point must be stressed again that his pioneering work in the name of the Baptist church took him to many parts of the Maritimes between 1784 and 1791, prior to his departure for Sierra Leone. His ministry included whites and blacks, a situation which caused considerable difficulty for him in the hostile racial climate of the day. At a time when travel was difficult and economic conditions harsh, David George undertook prayer-meeting tours to Saint John and Fredericton in New Brunswick and to many places in Nova Scotia, including Shelburne, Birchtown, Lockeport, Liverpool, Halifax and Preston.

The work of David George in the name of the Baptist Church in the Maritimes went beyond the call of spiritual work into alleviating the social conditions of his people. The records show that he interceded between white employers and black employees, seeking release for the latter to go to Sierra Leone. In this regard, John Clarkson, commissioner for the Sierra Leone Company in the Maritimes, owed much to David George's efforts on behalf of the black emigrants. Here, once again, was an example of the continuing responsibilities assumed by black Baptist church clergymen over the years for their congregations.

Birchtown was swept by a religious revival during the winter of

1784/85, and both King and his wife were converted to the Methodist Church by Moses Wilkinson, another Black Loyalist. Wilkinson's activities were nothing short of inspired, and even John Wesley was impressed by the enthusiasm of the Birchtown Blacks.

Following his conversion, King began preaching in black settlements from Shelburne to Halifax. Disenchanted with economic conditions in Shelburne, he and his wife left the area and in 1791 he was called to Preston as preacher to the black Methodists there. Although happy with his work in that community, King was particularly interested in spreading Christianity to the Blacks in Africa, and was instrumental in attracting emigrants for the migration to Sierra Leone in 1792, where he himself died in 1802. It was owing to King and other preachers like him that, by 1790, the Black Loyalists constituted one-quarter of the Methodists in Nova Scotia.

Thomas Peters must rank as the best known of the Black Loyalists. His futile efforts over a period of six years to obtain land for himself and his followers in Nova Scotia and New Brunswick, and his journey to London in 1791, have already been discussed. His work in recruiting emigrants for Sierra Leone stamped Peters as a shrewd and determined organizer and activist. He was, most certainly, an outstanding public figure in his time. The tragedy was that he succumbed to fever six months after leaving Nova Scotia. His place in Sierra Leone history, so ably described by that country's foremost historian, might well be his epitaph for his reputation in the Maritimes.

> Without his astonishing faith and courage in crossing the Atlantic to see the wrongs done to his people righted, no Nova Scotian settler would ever have come to Sierra Leone. Without the Nova Scotians the Colony could not have survived its first misfortunes. So in Thomas Peters we see, and should honour, one of its Founding Fathers.*

Moving from the founding fathers of the eighteenth century to the significant achievers and institutions of the nineteenth century, the most outstanding examples are Richard Preston as the church leader, and the African United Baptist Association as the formation of an important institution.

Richard Preston arrived in Halifax in either 1814 or 1815 with the

---

* C.H. Fyfe, "Thomas Peters: History and Legend" *Sierra Leone Studies*, No. 1, December, 1953, p. 13.

Richard Preston.

Black Refugees, to join his mother who had preceded him and who was then, unknown to him, living in the black settlement at Preston. He became a strong member of the Baptist Church in Halifax and in 1831 was sent to London to prepare for the ministry. He was duly ordained in May 1832 and returned to Halifax to assume charge of the African

United Baptist Church, Cornwallis Street, which was constituted on April 14, 1832. From then until his death in 1861, Richard Preston was the chief spokesman for the black Baptists in Nova Scotia.

Over a span of 21 years, he organized thirteen churches throughout the province. In 1854 he made his most important contribution when he convened a meeting of all black Baptist congregations in Nova Scotia to form a parent organization called the African United Baptist Association. In the 139 years of its existence to 1993, the AUBA has weathered many storms, has produced outstanding moderators and other office-bearers, and has introduced committees and programmes to respond to all needs and sectors of the black community. It has served, and continues to serve, as a provincial forum of considerable merit and potential.

There were others, too, whose life and work in religion remained as treasured memories for succeeding generations. Several accounts concerning them have already appeared, such as *A Brief History of the Coloured Baptists of Nova Scotia, 1782-1953* by Pearleen Oliver, and *From Generation to Generation, 1785-1985* by the same writer; *McKerrow, A Brief History of Blacks in Nova Scotia, 1783-1895*, introduced and edited by Frank Stanley Boyd, Jr., is another important source. As more local studies are completed, a fuller picture will appear.

The singular exception of a Maritime Black who achieved international fame outside the milieu of the church was William Hall who, in 1859, was awarded the Victoria Cross for outstanding bravery on November 10, 1857 with the British armed forces in the battle of Lucknow, India. He was the first Black, the first Nova Scotian and the first Canadian seaman to receive this high honour. According to a baptismal certificate located in Saint Andrews United Church, Wolfville, Nova Scotia, his birthdate is given as April 25, 1829 and the full name as William Neilson Hall. He was born in Horton Bluff near Wolfville. The name William Edward Hall appears on a memorial cairn on the grounds of the Hantsport Baptist Church and on a memorial tablet at the Cornwallis Street Baptist Church in Halifax. Hall first joined the American navy and later the British navy. Prior to service in India, he had been a seaman in the Crimean War, 1854-6. Hall retired to the family farm in Avonport in 1876 with his V.C. and the rank of Petty Officer First Class, unhonoured and unsung until he was noticed by the Duke of York (later King George V) on a visit to Nova Scotia in 1901. Hall died in 1904 and was buried in an unknown grave, again without any military honours. It was only in 1937 that members of the Canadian Legion started a campaign for just recognition to be accorded to this illustrious son of the Maritimes. Ten years later his body was re-buried on the lawn of the Hantsport Baptist Church. A monument was built over his grave bearing a hand-carved replica of the Victoria Cross. Other posthumous honours have followed belatedly: William Hall, V.C. Branch 57 of the Canadian Legion in Halifax was renamed after him; a gymnasium in Cornwallis and the Da Costa-Hall Educational program for black students in Montreal also perpetuate his memory. In 1986 the Nova Scotia Tattoo Gun Run was named after him.

Two black lawyers whose life and work spanned the late nineteenth and early twentieth centuries were Abraham B. Walker and James R. Johnston. Walker was born in British Columbia, took his law degree in the United States and moved to Saint John, New Brunswick in 1890. He was then the only black barrister in the Maritimes. Walker soon became involved in both political and early black activism. His experience with the political process reflects the dilemma facing the few educated Blacks at that time: the support they gave to political parties did not produce positive results for the black community; their votes seemed too marginal to matter. Although Walker appears to have been frustrated in his dealings with the Conservative Party prime minister, Sir Charles Tupper, in 1896, and with his Liberal successor, Sir Wilfred Laurier, he nevertheless remained in the background of mainstream politics.

Undaunted, he next founded a journal called *Neith* in Saint John in 1903. In its columns he gave vent to his other concerns: the disabilities suffered by black people and his strategy for redress. In this, he anticipated Marcus Garvey by advocating a back-to-Africa campaign and, like Garvey after him, received no support from Blacks for such a policy. Disappointed in his efforts in Saint John, in 1905 he moved to the United States where, like other Blacks, he was assured of better opportunities and a bigger audience. Indeed, in 1889 before coming to Saint John, this excellent orator and well-read scholar had undertaken a tour of the United States, where he spoke of his vision for the future. Walker's exhortation to his people in 1889 carried a special significance a hundred years later:

> We must produce great scientists, great scholars, great poets, great philosophers, great theologians, great statesmen, great journalists, great jurists and great reformers.
> We need men who can go to the very roots of things—that

is, men who can meet on equal terms, on any platform, the very best, men in the world*

The other lawyer was James Robinson Johnston, who was born in Halifax, Nova Scotia in 1877, and who graduated from Dalhousie University Law School in 1898, the first Black in the Maritimes to obtain a local law degree. He opened a law office in Halifax in 1900 at 197 Hollis Street and in 1908 moved to 58 Bedford Row. He was an excellent criminal lawyer who was referred to as the "Martin Luther King of Nova Scotia" by Barry Cahill, manuscripts archivist, Public Archives of Nova Scotia.† James R. Johnston was the first person of African descent to obtain a degree at Dalhousie University, the first to be admitted to the bar and only the third black barrister in all of Canada. The James Robinson Johnston Chair in Canadian Black Studies created at Dalhousie University in 1991 is a fitting tribute to the memory and the example of an outstanding Nova Scotian.

Before his legal career, Johnston was already an active member of the Cornwallis Street Baptist Church, where he held the positions of superintendent of the Sunday School, clerk of the church and president and organizer of the Black Youth Provincial Union. As a youth leader, committed activist and lawyer, Johnston was eminently qualified to assume the key position of Clerk of the African United Baptist Association in 1906. One of his objectives was to break down the prejudice that existed in rural black communities against post-secondary education. He proposed in 1905 to found a normal and industrial school on the model of the Hampton Institute in Virginia. Supported by the Rev. Moses B. Puryear, who had come to Nova Scotia in 1909 as pastor of the Cornwallis Street Baptist Church, the scheme was approved in 1914 and endorsed by civic and church leaders. In September 1915, the AUBA adopted a resolution that the proposed institution be known as the Industrial School of Nova Scotia for Coloured Children.

Johnston did not live to share in this resolution, or to see the little cottage in the north end of Halifax which served as the first school for three weeks, before it was blown up in the Halifax Explosion of 1917.

---

* A.B. Walker. The Negro Problem or the Philosophy of Race Development from a Canadian Standpoint (Atlanta, 1890), p.10.

† *Mail Star*, September 18, 1991. Barry Cahill has researched extensively on James R. Johnston and his work was published Fall, 1992 as "The 'Coloured Barrister': The Short Life and Tragic Death of James Robinson Johnston, 1876-1915" in the Dalhousie Law Journal, Vol. 15, No. 2

James Johnston.

He died on March 3, 1915, leaving behind a dream and a bequest, both of which still live on in the form of the Nova Scotia Home for Coloured Children, which was officially opened on June 6, 1921 on a 211-acre plot situated in Westphal, Halifax County.

The Nova Scotia Home for Coloured Children brings to mind the

Prominent Individuals and Institutions   39

James A. R. Kinney.

name of James A.R. Kinney, one of the leading Blacks in the Maritimes during the early twentieth century. Like Walker and Johnston, Kinney was interested in leading the black communities out of isolation and into the mainstream of Canadian society through education. Born in Yarmouth in 1878, Kinney was the first Black to graduate from the Maritime

The Home for Coloured Children.

Business College, in 1897. For 26 years he worked as advertising manager for William Stairs, Son and Morrow Company. He was a leading member of the AUBA, serving as its clerk from 1916 to 1921 and as its treasurer from 1939 to 1940. In these capacities, he was drawn into involvement with the Home for Coloured Children.

This Home, the only one of its kind in Canada, was begun to take care of black orphans and neglected children, to train them and to place them back into society. A farm had been started in order to raise money towards making the Home self-supporting, but was discontinued in 1946 because it was not economically viable, Two large gardens continued to grow produce for the Home itself. A school was run for a short time but, like the farm, was found to be unsuccessful.

During the Kinney years, from 1921 to 1940, the Home went through several crises-ridden periods as Blacks began to work out strategies for self-development, as opposed to strategies for integration. It was recognized, for example, that black children of whatever religious

Nova Scotia Home for Coloured Children as it appears today.

affiliation remained outside the pale of the common orphanages. Kinney was of the view that the Home should open its doors to all black children regardless of religion, and that the Home should exist as a separate black institution which would prepare its charges for the day when they would operate within the larger society on equal terms. A few objected to this segregationist approach and called for an integrationist strategy. It is interesting to note that this argument still divides the foundations of the Home. In 1973 the emphasis was shifted from an orphanage to a child development residential centre, and the former Home was duly incorporated as a Children's Aid Society for black children in Nova Scotia.

Two other personalities, contemporaries of Kinney, grappled with similar and related concerns. They were the Rev. Wellington Noey States and the Rev. William Andrew White. Wellington States was born in Wolfville, Nova Scotia in 1877. Having lost his parents at an early age, he was brought up by his white grandparents in Kingsport, in circumstances which compelled him to run away to sea and to return later to his father's family in Mount Denson. He later enrolled at Horton Academy, the forerunner of Acadia University, and the leading Baptist

Rev. Wellington States.

school in Nova Scotia. In 1898 he received a licence to preach at the Cornwallis Street Baptist Church in Halifax and in the following year was ordained. Between 1900 and 1905 he served in various parts of the province, including Granville Ferry, Delaps Cove, Hammonds Plains, Beech Hill, Cobequid Road and Falmouth. As field missionary for the AUBA, he was widely travelled and widely respected.

He married a distinguished daughter of John and Georgina States of Avonport in 1906, and a day later went to New Glasgow as the pastor of the Second United Baptist Church. There he founded the Nova Scotia Northern Association Convention, which included white churches supported by the Baptist Home Mission Board. After 13 years in New Glasgow, Rev. States took over as pastor of the Victoria Road Baptist Church and Cherrybrook Church in Dartmouth, where he served from 1919 till his death in 1927.

His wife Muriel Viola States, who lived on to 1984, earned a notable place for herself and her family in the annals of the black experience in the Maritimes. In her own right she served as president of the Victoria Road Baptist Ladies' Auxiliary for 40 years, and as organizer of the Ladies' Auxiliary of the AUBA for 38 years, for which she received wide public acclaim and many awards from her grateful community. The children of Wellington and Muriel States, now all deceased, achieved noteworthy heights during their lifetimes, inspired by the performance of successful parents.

The other personality, William Andrew White, a contemporary of Wellington States, has achieved for himself and his equally-distinguished children, a lasting place in Nova Scotia, Canadian and international history. Born in Virginia, White entered Acadia University to read theology in 1899. Upon graduating in 1903, he was appointed by the Baptist Home Mission Board to do missionary work in Nova Scotia. He organized the Second United Baptist Church in New Glasgow, and from 1905 to 1915 he served as pastor at the Truro Zion church.

In 1916 he was appointed chaplain of the No. 2 Construction Battalion, and was the only black chaplain in the British armed forces during the First World War. In 1919, Rev. White assumed his final position, as pastor of the Cornwallis Street Baptist Church in Halifax, where he achieved fame in many ways, including monthly radio broadcasts of his services to Canada and parts of the United States. In June 1936, Acadia University bestowed on him an honorary degree, in recognition of years of devoted service to the church and to his people.

Wellington States and Muriel States.

Prominent Individuals and Institutions   **45**

Dr. White died in September of the same year.

Thirteen children were born to William Andrew and Izie Dora White, three of whom died at a very early age. The rest went on to acquire an education and to carve out noteworthy careers when times were difficult for Blacks. The most distinguished of their children was the internationally-famous Portia White, who was born in Truro on June 24, 1911 and who died in Toronto on February 15, 1968. Portia was born into a family of accomplished musicians and singers and went on to become an opera star of world renown. After completing high school in Halifax, she began teaching at the age of 17 to earn a living. Her first big break came when, as a result of winning a silver cup at the Nova Scotia Music Festival, she gained a scholarship tenable at the Halifax Conservatory of Music. Her days of hardship, including severe financial difficulties, were overcome by hard work and long hours, spurred on by an ambition to succeed.

At her death, Portia White had achieved a greater international fame than any other Canadian Black. Her success was partly due to the changing racial and political climate during the years that marked her greatest achievements (1941 to 1968). These were precisely the years when racial prejudice and discrimination were beginning to be overcome as a result of national and international developments. These years also saw significant changes taking place in the Maritimes, as new political organizations emerged and new leaders appeared on the scene. It was during this period that new foundations were laid for the marked improvements which have become noticeable in the 1980s and the 1990s.

In Nova Scotia, the most notable contemporary personality, and one whose name is associated with every important development that has taken place in the black community during these last five decades, is undoubtedly the Rev. Dr. William Pearly Oliver. Born on February 11, 1912 in Wolfville, William Oliver received his education from elementary school through high school to university in Wolfville, through the integrated system obtained in that town. He realized, however, in his teenage years that the society which had previously opened its doors to him in the common school, common church, common Sunday School, common scouting, sporting and club facilities, was not quite prepared to keep the door open for him in later years. The lesson was clear: Blacks had to work out their own permanent salvation in their own setting, using positive self-pride and powerful cultural awareness as props for survival

Beechville Baptist Church.

and advancement.

The holder of two university degrees (1934 and 1936) and the recipient of two honorary doctoral degrees (1964, 1977), Dr. Oliver was the founder and guiding spirit of the Nova Scotia Association for the Advancement of Coloured Peoples (NSAACP), the Black United Front (BUF) and the Society for the Protection and Preservation of Black Culture in Nova Scotia, known in short as the Black Cultural Society for Nova Scotia. These later developments came after a lifetime of dedicated and innovative service to the Windsor Plains African Baptist Church (1936/37), the Cornwallis Street African Baptist Church (1937-1962), and the Beechville and Cobequid Road Baptist Churches (1937 to 1989). Dr. Oliver served the AUBA in many positions, including moderator in 1962. In 1960 he was elected president of the United Baptist Convention of the Maritimes. Outside the structure of the church, he worked from 1962 to 1977 as a regional representative with the Adult Education Division of the Nova Scotia Department of Education. In 1984 he received the Order of Canada; in 1985, the Human Relations Award from the Canadian Council of Christians and Jews and in 1988 the Distinguished Service Award of the Alumni of Acadia

William Pearly and Mrs. Oliver.

Black Cultural Centre

University. Dr. William Pearly Oliver died on May 26, 1989.

In 1936 William Oliver married the former Pearleen Borden, who has stood out in her own right as a devoted and accomplished church worker, rising to the position of moderator of the AUBA from 1976 to 1978, the first woman ever to hold this position. The marriage was blessed with five sons, all of whom obtained at least one university degree, in some cases more, and in one instance a doctoral degree—a remarkable achievement by any standard.

Pearleen Oliver has herself made a significant contribution to scholarship, church life and community development. She has devoted more than 50 years as a researcher, author, historian, public speaker and human rights leader. Born in New Glasgow in 1917, Pearleen Borden was the first black student to graduate from New Glasgow High School in 1936. Later that year she married Reverend W.P. Oliver and from that year until the death of her husband in 1989, the Olivers made up a marvelous team serving the same institutions and organizations.

Pearleen Oliver is a foremost historian of the black experience in Nova Scotia, particularly in the field of church-related community history. She was the first woman to be elected moderator of the African United Baptist Association of Nova Scotia in 1976 and received the first Woman of the Year Award from YWCA in 1981. In October, 1990, she received an Honorary Doctor of Letters degree from Saint Mary's University, Halifax.

The Olivers' life and work most be considered alongside the institutions they have helped to establish. The NSAACP was founded in 1945 to serve as a provincial body to improve and further the interests of the black people of Nova Scotia. Though the membership has never been large, over the years the NSAACP served to articulate the grievances of black people until other organizations came into existence. It took up the case for Blacks attempting to enter the nursing profession, and it took cases of racial discrimination to court, most notably that of Mrs. Viola Desmond. The fact that the Nova Scotia government passed the Fair Employment Practices Act in 1955 and the Fair Accommodations Act in 1959 was due in no small measure to the protests initiated and publicized by the NSAACP. Though later labelled conservative in outlook and outmoded in strategy, the role of the NSAACP must be assessed in the light of the available options and platforms at that time.

Various accounts of these limited options have been chronicled in Carrie M. Best's book, entitled *That Lonesome Road*. This author also deserves a special place in the history of Blacks in the Maritimes. Born in New Glasgow, Nova Scotia, in 1903, Carrie Best became involved in community affairs at a young age. In 1946 she began publication of a newspaper called *The Clarion*, later changed to *The Negro Citizen*, which continued to 1956. In 1975 she was awarded an honorary doctorate by Saint Francis Xavier University, the first black woman in the Maritimes to be so honoured. In 1985 this distinction was shared by Marie Hamilton of Halifax, who was honoured by Mount Saint Vincent University for her outstanding contribution to the enhancement of community life.

Carrie M. Best pioneered journalism in the black community. Long before starting her own newspaper, *The Clarion*, on July 26, 1946, she was a contributor to the first black newspaper, *The Nova Scotia Gleaner*, founded by black lawyer, Allan Hamilton, in 1929 in Sydney, Cape Breton. Her autobiography, *That Lonesome Road* was published in 1977. Her son, Calbert James Best, was the first black Nova Scotian to

Dr. Carrie M. Best. O.C. founder of **The Clarion.**

obtain a diploma in Journalism from Kings University College. He was a regular columnist in his mother's newspaper before joining the federal service where he rose to the rank of Canadian High Commissioner to Trinidad and Tobago in 1985—an additional first for a black Nova Scotian.

No short history can do justice to the numerous prominent individuals who have contributed significantly to black history, culture and society in the Maritimes. While only a sampling can be presented in the present study, it is clear that this sector of the Maritime population has produced many success stories. Some have been recounted; others will now follow.

Charles Ernest Ryan is a legend in Prince Edward Island. Born in Charlottetown on July 11, 1918, Charles Ryan began his baseball career with the Canadians in the Charlottetown Junior League in the 1930s. After military service in World War II, he returned to the Maritimes in 1945 and resumed his baseball career as a leading first baseman, and an all star catcher and pitcher. He played with the Dartmouth Arrows Club in the Halifax District semi-professional league, then with the Anchors of the Charlottetown League and the Charlottetown Abbies at the provincial and Maritime levels. When his remarkable playing days were over, Prince Edward Island's popularly known "Mr. Baseball" became recreation director for the City of Charlottetown from 1966 to 1989, a position he served with equal distinction. After his death on November 9, 1989, the Charlottetown Baseball League was renamed the Charles Ryan Memorial Baseball League. Three years before his death, he was inducted in the Prince Edward Island Sports Hall of Fame—a far cry from the Island's eighteenth century view of its black citizens.

An outstanding sportsman, administrator, educator and community activist in New Brunswick—three years older than Charles Ryan—is Clifford Skinner. A graduate of the Saint John Vocational School in 1934, Clifford Skinner served the Canadian Army for three years between 1939 and 1942 and then opened his own business called Nick's Welding and Ornamental Iron Works, an enterprise which he ran for 17 years. Clifford Skinner was a founding member of the Colour Progressive Association in 1943, the Provincial Resources of Black Energy (PROBE) in 1969 and PRUDE—a New Brunswick black organization mentioned in earlier pages—and has devoted a lifetime promoting the Canadian Football League, Track and Field, Basketball, Coaching and Gymnastics in many areas of which he excelled in his youth and passed on to other members of his family, one of whom, Chris Skinner, played running back for the Edmonton Eskimos.

This remarkable athlete was the holder of five records simultaneously with the Saint John Schoolboy Track and Field Association—four of which he established on a single day in 1932 (100 yards, high jump, broad jump and relay—the broad jump record of 19 feet 3 1/2 inches stood unbroken for 25 years).

Between 1985 and 1992, Clifford Skinner worked hard to forge the

Clifford Skinner.

links between Black Maritimers and the descendants of the Black Loyalists who emigrated to Sierra Leone, West Africa in 1792 and to celebrate the Sierra Leone, Nova Scotia and New Brunswick connections, a celebration which culminated with a visit by Black Maritimers to Freetown, Sierra Leone, in 1992.

In the account of prominent Black Maritimers a significant feature is the story of prominent families. Further studies will show that the influence of the family environment, the family collective and the family strengths contributed substantially to the achievements of family members. Conversely, the breakdown of the family has been recognized by church leaders, social workers, educators and institutions as a contributing factor in the 1980s and the 1990s to indifference in the work ethics, school dropouts, incidents of anti-social behaviour and decline in family values. While declining economic opportunities and the continuing prevalence of racism in society in the 1980s and the 1990s are contributing factors that cannot be ignored, they cannot be considered to be the exclusive factors that obstruct progress.

Reference has already been made to the Skinner family of New Brunswick. In Prince Edward Island, the Byers family is an example. William Byers, a slave, was born in 1789. He later headed a household of eighteen persons, became Charlottetown's first licensed chimney sweep, was once facetiously nominated for mayor but actually came "within a hair's breadth of being His Worship Mayor Byers."* His sons and grandsons worked as labourers, fishermen or longshoremen, the only opportunities at the time, except in the squared rings where black boxers defied all odds—a story mentioned later in this section.

In Nova Scotia, the family of Reverend Dr. William Andrew White is remembered as an outstanding family which has contributed to the church, the army, education, pharmacy, music, community development and cross-cultural understanding. Reverend White, Portia White and Lorne White appear in many chronicles in Maritime history.

The Paris families of New Glasgow have achieved numerous distinctions as have the Bordens of the same town. Dr. Peter Paris, Elmer G. Homrighausen Professor of Christian Social Ethics, Princeton Theological Seminary, New Jersey, USA is the eldest in the family of ten children. A number of firsts belong to this Nova Scotian: the first black Canadian to obtain the Ph.D. in religion, the first to receive graduate degrees from the University of Chicago, the first to teach at Howard University, the first to reach the rank of Full Professor at Vanderbilt

* Cited in Jim Hornby, *Black Islanders*, p. 95.

George Borden.

University, Nashville and the first to hold his present rank at Princeton. His sister, Cherry M. Paris has held the position of Regional Supervisor,

Walter Borden.

Nova Scotia Human Rights Commission in its Digby office for many years while another sister, Beverly Bonvie works for the same Commission in its New Glasgow office. A third sister, Gloria, is a senior employee of Scott Maritime, Pictou.

There are many Bordens who feature among New Glasgow's legacy to the Maritimes. With a strong military background comes Captain George Borden who retired in 1985 after a career of 32 years. In 1986 he served as Executive Assistant to the Minister of Community Services and was the first black Nova Scotian to hold that office. George Borden's first work of cultural poetry C*anaan Odyssey* was published in 1988 while his second book *Footprints, Images and Reflections* was published in 1993.

George's brother, Walter Borden, has earned a reputation as an outstanding actor. Between 1986 and 1992, Walter Borden has performed in numerous radio dramas and stage and television plays. His performances in Tar*tuffe, Shineboy, Tightrope Time, God's Trombones, Gideon's Blues, Miss Daisy, Hamlet* and *Shylock*, among others received unrivalled acclamation and confirmed him as the Maritime's finest talent in his field.

A younger Borden, also from New Glasgow, Marion Aretha Borden, is making a name for herself in the religious, social and cultural fields. Holder of a Master's degree in Divinity in 1992, this young student pastor is on her way up the theological ladder of the Black Baptist Church which has yet to ordain a woman in Nova Scotia. Licentiate Borden has the credential which are strengthened by an impressive array of professional memberships and extracurricular activities between 1983 and 1993.

Sydney, Nova Scotia, holds its own ground with distinction. It was here that Allan Hamilton, graduate of Dalhousie University Law School, opened a law practice in 1922, started the first black newspaper in 1929, and became the first black Canadian to be elevated to the rank of King's Counsel in 1950. Six years later, Sydney produced the first black alderman east of Montreal when Thomas Miller was elected to the Sydney City Council, a position he held for 17 years. Alderman Miller died on January 20, 1987.

Two distinguished members of the Ruck family add to the Sydney origins and contributions. The older brother, Winston Spencer Ruck, who died on August 15, 1992, made a remarkable contribution to Maritime history and society. The obituary headlines in newspapers captured the essence of his greatness: "Ruck remembered as diplomat who won respect"; "Our differences are small"; "Province loses 'positive force'".

*Winston Ruck, former secretary of the Sydney Steelworkers Union
and Director of the Black United Front. (Died August 15, 1992).*

Winston Ruck began his working life at age 17 in the Sydney Steel
Plant where he served for 37 years. In 1970 he was elected president of
the United Steel Workers of America, Local 1064, a position to which
he was elected twice. He was district representative of the union for 14
years. He retired in 1987 and in 1989 was named Executive Director of

Prominent Individuals and Institutions   57

Calvin W. Ruck, author of Canada's Black Battalion No. 2 Construction.

---

* *Cape Breton Magazine*, No. 60, June 1992 published an extensive interview with Winston Ruck.

58   Blacks

the Black United Front of Nova Scotia, a position he vacated the same year owing to ill health. He was a board member of the Nova Scotia Rehabilitation Centre as well as the Black Cultural Society. An honorary citizen of Sydney and winner of the Tom Miller Human Rights Award in 1990, Winston Ruck preached and practised the gospel of membership of the human family. While accepting the Tom Miller award he said: "Those in authority have to reach out to all minorities and bring them into the fold. There must be the political will. We're all brothers and sisters, we have more in common than not in common. Our differences are small."*

Younger brother Calvin Ruck, continues the work in the Halifax-Dartmouth Metro and County areas of Nova Scotia since leaving his birthplace in Sydney in 1945. Over the next four decades, he advanced his education and his careers in many fields: community service worker in the Nova Scotia Department of Social Services, family benefits worker in Halifax and Dartmouth and Human Rights Officer of the Nova Scotia Human Rights Commission, retiring in 1986. Soon after, he was appointed Commissioner and in 1991 elected vice-chair of the Human Rights Commission. He was one of the early members of the following organizations which he has continued to serve over the years: the Nova Scotia Association for the Advancement of Coloured People; the North Preston Daycare Medical Society; the Black Cultural Society of Nova Scotia, the Preston Lions Club and the deacon's board of his church. Author of C*anada's Black Battalion: No. 2 Construction, 1916-1920*, Calvin Ruck is now working on a book on Blacks in the Second World War. He received the prestigious Harry Jerome Award on March 14, 1987.

Black lawyers, doctors, nurses, civil service employees, teachers, principals, administrators, business persons, university professors and officers are to be found in every province of the Maritimes to a greater or lesser degree as one surveys the contemporary scene in the 1980s and the 1990s. They are all prominent individuals in their own right. Local and regional studies should highlight these categories so as to put to rest the emphasis on the absence of role models to inspire further progress.

This chapter will close with an overview of the black boxing fraternity in the Maritimes, a sector of the black experience that continues to dignify the courage, the discipline and the accomplishments of determined individuals to overcome odds and structured barriers. Every now and then the glory of the past comes back to life as

September 23, 1982. World War One Veterans Reunion and Recognition Banquet Advisory Committee, l-r: Isaac Phills, Calvin Ruck, chairperson, Charles Wilson, Deacon Sydney Jones. Photo taken at the Age & Opportunity Centre, Cornwallis Street, Halifax, NS.

Black Cultural Centre

was exemplified on June 6, 1992, when a great Nova Scotian Black, born in Weymouth Falls, Sam Langford, who died in 1956, was the subject of the dedication of a memorial plaque at the Weymouth Falls Community Centre—a centre which is now named after him. Prominent black columnist Charles Saunders, author of *Sweat and Soul. The Saga of Black Boxers From The Halifax Forum to Caesar's Palace* had this to say on the occasion of the June 6, 1992 dedication: "It is difficult for us today to imagine Sam Langford's world: the world of this century's first twenty years. Basic human rights we take for granted today were only a dream back then. Black people's aspirations crashed daily against a wall built of intolerance and indifference.

Yet Blacks struggled to shatter that wall, brick by brick. Some battles were small, others large and sweeping. The most spectacular and visible of those battles were fought within the confines of the boxing ring."*

* *The Sunday Daily News*, June 14, 1992.

Another occasion was the Black Boxers Reunion and Remembrance Night on October 1, 1988, organized by the Black Cultural Centre for Nova Scotia and spearheaded by Delmore Buddy Daye, a former Canadian boxing champion and comprising Ricky Anderson, another Canadian boxing champion, Murray Langford, relative of Sam Langford and a distinguished boxing coach, Henry Bishop, Curator of the Black Cultural Centre and the writer-then executive director of the Black Cultural Centre.

The occasion paid tribute to former Maritime boxers whose accomplishments adorned the boxing ring all over the Maritimes and beyond for many decades, some no longer alive, names such as Sam Langford, George Dixon, Tiger Warrington, Jesse Elroy Mitchell, Ricky Anderson, Dexter Connors, Delmore Buddy Daye, Dave Downey, Ozzie Farrell, Donnie Johnson, Leroy Jones, Leroy Lawrence, Sherrie Lawrence, Cecil Gray, Clyde Gray, Roy Hamilton, Poole Izzard, Jojo Jackson, Archie Lee, George Munro, Keith Paris, Percy Paris, Joe Pyle, Allison Sparks, Arnold Sparks, Len Sparks, Lawrence States and Bryan Gibson. The younger generation was represented by Raymond Downey and Kirk Johnson who have continued to make their marks on the contemporary boxing scene.

The remarkable side of this memorable event was that all the names mentioned , living and dead, were black Nova Scotians who fought their way to hard-won victories, defying segregated living and segregated opportunities, through sheer mental and physical discipline. Following this event, Charles Saunders captured the essence of this discipline in his book S*weat and Soul. The Saga of Black Boxers From The Halifax Forum to Caesar's Palace*:

> "From small communities established two centuries ago on the shores of the Atlantic, black boxers such as George Dixon, Sam Langford and Clyde Gray have reached the top of their profession. Others have toiled in the trenches, trading blood and pain for a couple of wrinkled dollars and the opportunity to do it all over again a few days or weeks later.
>
> Big men, small men, champions, near champions, contenders, or preliminary fighters . . . Blacks from Nova Scotia, New Brunswick and Prince Edward Island have filled these niches in rings around the world. Whatever the level to which their talent and circumstances have carried them, they have always battled with honor and distinction."*

* S*weat and Soul*, p. 11.

The New Brunswickers mentioned in the book are Howard Leslie of Saint John who later moved to Ontario and founded the musical group "The Lincolns" when his fighting days were over; Crosby Irvine who stayed on in Saint John; Carl White who fought in the 1940s and 1950s and went on to become a committed black community activist and President of PRUDE—mentioned in earlier pages—Percy "Turk" Richard. All these black New Brunswickers were inspired by an earlier generation spearheaded by Ray McIntyre and Cecil Braithwaite, both of Saint John.

Black Prince Edward Islanders are led in this field by George Godfrey and George Byers who fought during the last decades of the nineteenth century. Byers moved to Boston from Charlottetown, fought world champions, as Sam Langford and George Dixon of Nova Scotia did, and started a boxing school. One of his pupils was a black islander named George DeCoursey. But his prize pupil was Sam Langford. What a combination this Maritime team of George Byers and Sam Langford made. As trainer and pugilist this team went on a memorable British tour in 1911. Sam Langford paid Byers the finest tribute in his autobiography which appeared in the *Halifax Evening Mail* in August-September, 1924:

> "I've forgotten many things in the years since then, but I've
> never forgotten the things George taught me or the advice he
> gave me way back in 1902 when I was 16 and just beginning
> a 23-year career in the prize ring."*

Other black Islanders of boxing fame were the Ryan brothers, Dick and Stanley "Tucker, the Claybourne brothers, Philip, Mark and Tommy, and the Gallants, Al and "Bub"; Benny Benns and Bill Pryor. The last named fought under the name "Billy the Kid"; later became a judge for the Halifax Boxing Commission and was inducted in the Canadian Boxing Hall of Fame in 1976.

What the story of black boxers, other sports personalities, community and church leaders reveals is the courage which spurred them on and the contribution their efforts made to society as a whole, not to Blacks alone, but to the total society. It is this story, in the words of Charles Saunders of "small communities," of those who "toiled in the trenches," of "big men, small men, champions, near champions" which needs to be further researched and further told and re-told, for the story of black Maritimers is one of courage personified.

* Charles Saunders, *Sweat and Soul*, p. 79.

CHAPTER 5

Blacks in the Maritimes in the Early 1980's

I. New Directions

The late 1960s was a time of ferment among Blacks throughout the world, as more and more of their brethren in Africa regained independence from European colonial rule. The civil rights movement gained increased intensity in the United States and some of this spilt over into Canada and the Maritimes. On November 30, 1968 an interim committee was struck at a Black Panthers' meeting in Halifax under the chairmanship of Dr. Oliver, to design the structure of a political organization to represent black interests and aspirations in Nova Scotia. The result was the formation of the Black United Front in 1969 to bring Blacks closer to the realization of their objectives: to reach economic, political and social power. From 1969 to the mid-1980s, the BUF has enjoyed an uneven passage. Under three executive directors during this period (Jules Oliver, Arthur Criss—later known as Haamid Rasheed—and Richard Joseph, and one interim director Captain George Borden), the organization nevertheless survived and remained active. For as long as Blacks in Nova Scotia remain on the periphery of mainstream society, it will have an important part to play as an advocacy organization.

The third and last organization associated with the life and work of Dr. William Oliver is the Black Cultural Society for Nova Scotia. Dr. Oliver long grappled with the fundamental issue of black advancement. He came to the conclusion that no amount of education, wealth or political power was worth anything unless and until a deep sense of pride, identity and cultural awareness was inculcated among Blacks. Once this was achieved, they would begin to enjoy all the different manifestations of progress. To realize this objective, in 1972 Dr. Oliver proposed that the Society should set up a Black Cultural Education Centre (later shortened to Black Cultural Centre) to provide an oppor-

The Black Cultural Centre.

tunity for black people "to learn about themselves, and concurrently for other groups to learn about black people . . . ". From 1972 to 1983, the proposal became a reality: the Society for the Protection and Preservation of Black Culture in Nova Scotia was incorporated in 1977; and $1.2 million was raised to build the Black Cultural Centre, which was officially opened on September 17, 1983. Its foundation president was Donald H. Oliver, Q.C., one of the foremost black lawyers in the Maritimes. Dr. William Oliver, its guiding spirit, held the office of honorary president. The president in 1985 was H.A. Wedderburn, another prominent black lawyer who has served for some 25 years as the president of the NSAACP.

In April 1985, the Black Cultural Centre embarked on an expanded scale of activities to realize its objectives of making the Centre a vibrant cultural institution. A well-known black civil servant and municipal councillor, Wayne Adams, was appointed executive director and a prominent Africanist, author and professor of History, Dr. Bridglal Pachai, was named programme director. The founding curator of the Centre, Henry Bishop, managed to put together a museum which depicts

Donald H. Oliver.

most graphically aspects of the Nova Scotian black experience in pictures, photographs, artifacts and documents. This Centre, the only one of its kind in Canada, stands as an inspiring symbol of the black people's search for self-respect, pride in race, loyalty to God and country, and quest for justice, equality and advancement. In 1989, Dr. Pachai left the Centre which he had served as Executive Director since

Blacks in the Maritimes in the Early 1980s   65

H. A. J. Wedderburn.

F. D. Hodges.

1986 to assume the position of Executive Director of the Nova Scotia Human Rights Commission. Councillor Wayne Adams returned in 1989 to his previous position. The later history of the Centre appears in Chapter 6.

Other institutions, organizations and individuals, too, in the period since 1941 have made their contributions felt in the cause of advancement of Blacks in the Maritimes. Notable among these are the New Brunswick Association for the Advancement of Coloured People (formed in 1959), the New Brunswick Human Rights Commission (1967) and the Nova Scotia Human Rights Commission (1967). The founding members of the New Brunswick Association for the Advancement of Coloured People deserve special mention: Walter Peters, Fred Hodges, Joe Drummond, Garfield Skinner and Ovid Machett.

Joseph Drummond was born on April 7, 1926 and died on January 13, 1975. In his short but full life he championed the cause of black identity and black progress. Three years before his death he called for a history of the Blacks to be told in all its richness and variety. He particularly lamented the ridicule directed towards Blacks by western civilization: the age-old taunt, "You are nothing. You are niggers". Drummond served for several terms as vice-president of the National Black Coalition, formed in 1969. In 1971, he received a scroll of commendation from the city of Saint John in recognition of his public work and his appointment as a member of the Human Rights Commission.

In 1984 the University of New Brunswick accorded Frederick Douglas Hodges, a Saint John labour leader, the honorary degree of doctor of laws. Hodges was born and educated in Saint John, served in the Royal Canadian Air Force as a radio and telephone operator, and had a long career with the Canadian Pacific Railway. He served for ten years as president of the Saint John District Labour Council and for three years as vice-president of the New Brunswick Federation of Labour. He was the first Black to be elected to public office in Saint John, when he served a three-year term as city councillor.

An important contemporary organization set up in 1980 and incorporated in 1981 to serve the black community of New Brunswick is PRUDE (Pride of Race, Unity and Dignity through Education). Its aims are to promote cultural identity through education and through local and provincial activities stressing black culture, heritage and religion. PRUDE also monitors the needs of Blacks and promotes activities, discussions and programmes aimed at enhancement of cultural standards and resolution of problems, as well as advising on job opportunities for members of the black community. Its current president is Carl A. White, Jr. An organization of related objectives in Nova Scotia is the Watershed Association Development Enterprise (WADE) which was incorporated in March 1984. It serves the largest concentration of Blacks in the Maritimes, in the communities of Cherrybrook/Lake Loon, Lake Major, North Preston and East Preston in Halifax County.

II. Problems

Organizations like PRUDE ad WADE face a formidable task in the 1980s and beyond to raise the social and economic standards of Blacks in the Maritimes. While it is true that there were some ten black lawyers in Nova Scotia in 1985; four holders of elected local government positions, including that of mayor held by Daurene Lewis of Annapolis Royal; two black directors of the Nova Scotia Human Rights Commission in the period 1971 to 1985 (Dr. George McCurdy and his successor, Dr. Anthony P. Johnstone*); a few women members holding senior

Daurene Lewis.

Wamboldt-Waterfield

---

* Deceased in 1990 and 1989 respectively.

Paul Anthony Johnstone.

federal government positions; a small number of black teachers, including a few vice-principals and one principal; and a number of distinguished and well-qualified church leaders throughout the Maritimes, these all pale into woeful insignificance when one considers the high rate of unemployment among Blacks, compounded by a large incidence of under-employment.

Statistics are hard to produce but the visible realities are clear. In the Preston area of Nova Scotia, some observers placed the percentage of unemployed in 1985 as high as 70 percent. According to one demographic survey conducted in New Brunswick in 1981, the unemployment figure for the black population there stood at 59 percent. In a report prepared by J. Wilkie Darisme in 1982 and entitled "Race Relations and Discrimination in the City of Saint John", it was noted that black people in that city continue to be the victims of prejudice and racial discrimination in housing, employment and public places. This re-echoes the familiar refrain sounded repeatedly for two hundred years.

The same holds true for the rest of the Maritimes. The picture is bleak but not hopeless. Black organizations and black leaders are responding to the challenges that still exist. They have behind them a long list of inspiring leaders who have served the black communities in the past. These men and women—some mentioned in this article and some omitted through constraints of space—lived, worked and died, some of them long since, when times were harder and opportunities fewer.

Notable sportsman, too, of past and present vintage have, through their achievements, done more for black pride and dignity than have some organizations and leaders. Among the notables in the first generation were George Dixon, Sam Langford, Jesse Elroy Mitchell and Terrence Warrington. Of the later generation, the notables have been Delmore William "Buddy" Daye, Stan Maxwell, Wayne Smith, Clyde Gray, David Downey, Kevin and Donnie Downey, and Ricky Anderson (who lost his Canadian welterweight crown in July 1985). The outstanding football player and athlete of the 1950s, Walter "Bubbles" Peters, now Major Walter Peters, brought great distinction through his outstanding prowess on the playing field. Born in Litchfield, New Brunswick, he earned his prominence in later years in Saint John, New Brunswick. While these achievements are remarkable and a matter of pride, they have also unfortunately served to reinforce a convenient western stereotype of Blacks: the harsh but oft-repeated slur that they are cut out only for matters of brawn rather than brain.

Black businesses, too, have had their difficult times. The rural craftspersons of old have all but disappeared. The petty traders have been overcome by current trends of capital and high technology. The Black Business Consortium Society of Nova Scotia exists to provide management consulting services to clients. The objectives are commendable, but the clientele remains small and few successful businesses have yet emerged. The Simmons Paving Company is one good example

GEORGE DIXON.

George Dixon.

Sam Langford.

Blacks in the Maritimes in the Early 1980s

of an enterprise which has survived for ten years since 1975. Looking back over this period, the president of the company, Wilfred Simmons, says:

> We have worked long and hard hours. We started with a crew of six, myself, my wife and four sons. We now have a crew of sixteen. Fourteen men and two women. We would like to consider our company successful. Our quality work speaks for itself. Our good fortune has been with the help of the Lord, a good wife, a devoted family and a multitude of good friends and fellow workers.

These words are redolent of the cry of the community spirit of old, which produced that sterling brand of church leaders, their devoted spouses and faithful followers. But the Maritimes—and the Canada—of the 1980s and beyond will provide less opportunity for such community advancement. Then there was the pervasive rationalization, based on racial grounds, that Blacks were different, inferior, and should be segregated. That rationalization no longer exists.

III. Prospects

In the wake of post-1971 multiculturalism and the 1982 Charter of Rights and Freedoms, a new era has opened for Blacks in the Maritimes and elsewhere. They, too, must now take their place as equal members in the mainstream of Canadian life. For this to happen with justice and dignity, there are rights and obligations that rest on Blacks themselves, on all tiers of government, and on fellow Canadians. It is no longer a secret that this needs to be done, and quickly. In the words of the House of Commons Report of the Special Committee on Visible Minorities in Canadian Society, dated March 1984 and entitled *Equality Now*, the issue is acknowledged with clarity:

> Full participation for visible minorities will be achieved when they are represented in the full spectrum of economic, political, social and cultural life of this country. There will be full equality for all individuals and mechanisms to ensure protection from all forms of discrimination.

When this objective is realized a new chapter will be written in the story of Blacks in the Maritimes. In the meantime, the remaining years of this century will be a crucial testing time, during which the determination and industry of Blacks themselves, the goodwill and contribution of fellow Canadians, and the sincerity and resolve of government, will all be on trial.

CHAPTER 6

Blacks in the Maritimes in the Later 1980s and Early 1990s

I. The Road to the 1990s

The decade ending in mid-1993 marked a time of considerable activity among black Maritimers, matched by mixed results.

In Nova Scotia particularly, where the largest number of black Maritimers live, progress—or movements towards progress—was quite remarkable. This can be measured by the heightened activities of a large number of organizations; responses to public issues of racism; emergence of significant publications; new and young faces on the scene and the quest for the power of politics.

Before 1945, organizations serving black Nova Scotians were few and far between: the African United Baptist Association (1854) and its affiliate churches of the nineteenth and twentieth centuries; the Halifax Coloured Citizens Improvement League (1932) and the Coloured Education Centre (1938).

Then came the Nova Scotia Association for the Advancement of Coloured People, incorporated on 29 March, 1945. Until the late 1960s nothing of significance was added to the list until the effects of world politics in the 1960s spilled over into American, Canadian and Nova Scotian politics—the emergence of new nation states in Africa, the Civil Rights Movement in America led by Reverend Dr. Martin Luther King till his assassination in 1968, English-French conflict in Canada, the appearance of the Black Panthers in Halifax in October-November 1968, signalling fears of black power militancy. Canadian politicians responded to this complex scene of varying proportions in different ways: the Canadian Bill of Rights made its appearance; the various Reports of the Royal Commission on Bilingualism and Biculturalism

Robert Upshaw, one-time executive director, Black Educators Association. Presently executive director of Black Learners Advisory Committee.

appeared, in the aftermath of which Canadian Multiculturalism policy was born.

In the very midst of all these events in different places and at different levels, the Black United Front of Nova Scotia came into existence in November, 1968. Several of its founding members have passed on but a few are still active in other ways in 1992-93: Burnley "Rocky" Jones, a lawyer in 1993; H.A.J. Wedderburn, a lawyer and President of NSAACP in 1993; Arnold Johnson, prominent black community leader in North Preston in 1993; Keith Prevost, prominent businessman in 1993; Churchill Smith, prominent church leader in 1993; Edith Gray, retired Halifax resident in 1993.

Those who are deceased in this group of founding members are Reverend W.P. Oliver and Ross Kinney. Its interim chairman, Dr. W.P. Oliver, spoke of the Black United Front as an umbrella for the black

Brad Barton, former principal, C.P. Allen High School. Presently supervisor of Race Relations, Cross Cultural Understanding and Race Relations, Halifax County Bedford District School Board.

family, a concept that has yet to reach fruition but one which continues to be held. The fact that BUF still exists in 1993, still continues to advocate the cause of black advancement, still has a part to play in spite of the proliferation of black organizations, underlines its usefulness on

Janis Jones-Darrell.

the Nova Scotia scene. With stability and with an agenda that would keep up with changing times, its role could be vital.

Many other black organizations now co-exist. Some would argue that there are far too many serving a single constituency where members have shrunk markedly, while others hold that in an age of daunting specializations there is enough room and justification for specialized services.

The Black Educators Association has been a powerful social force since 1969, providing a forum for black students, parents and teachers while serving in a liaison role between them and the government. Its three Executive Directors since August 1988—positions filled by practising black teachers on secondment—were Gerald Clarke, Robert Upshaw and Jocelyn Dorrington. Among those who have served this organization over the years as president are such names as H.A.J. (Gus) Wedderburn, Brad Barton, Gerald Clarke, Rev. Anna Hunter, Patricia Barton, Gertrude Tynes and Sheila Cole. In 1993, Brad Barton holds the position of Supervisor of Race Relations. Cross-Cultural Understanding and Human Rights with the Halifax County-Bedford District School Board. This is the first such position in Nova Scotia. It was created in 1991 and the first holder of this office was Janis Jones-Darrell, a leading black educator in Nova Scotia who, in 1993, was seconded as Consultant in this field to the Nova Scotia Department of Education. Gerald Clarke is principal of Halifax West Junior High School.

It is significant that in 1991 the Province of Nova Scotia created the Black Learners Advisory Committee after months of consultations between Delmore Buddy Daye and the Minister of Advanced Education and Job Training, Joel Matheson, Q.C. and his deputy Joseph Clarke. Delmore Daye chaired the committee in its initial days after which it was headed by Castor Williams, a black lawyer. Its first Executive Director was Robert Upshaw who moved to this position from the Black Educators Association.

Education for black students in Nova Scotia appears to be promising not only because of the dedicated work of the organizations mentioned but also because of positive responses from all levels of government and other institutions such as school boards, universities, the Nova Scotia Teachers Union as well as such programs as the Indigenous Black and Native Micmac Law Program, and the Transition Year Program at Dalhousie University and special scholarships and incentives.

The challenge to black parents and students is how best to utilize the educational opportunities that have become increasingly available in the 1980s and the 1990s.

Blacks in the Maritimes in the Later 1980s and Early 1990s   **79**

Delmore "Buddy" Daye.

One organization that was set up to protect and preserve black culture in Nova Scotia has made considerable progress since its formation mentioned in an earlier section. The Black Cultural Society (1977) is the parent body of the Black Cultural Centre (1983). Since its inception, the Society has been headed by notable black Nova Scotians in the following order up to 1993: Donald Oliver, H.A.J. Wedderburn,

Geraldine Browning, Ruth Johnson, Alma Johnston and Anne Simmons. The Executive Directors of the Black Cultural Centre between 1983 and 1993 were Frank Boyd, Bridglal Pachai and Wayne Adams. The Black Cultural Centre is unique in Canada, located in the very heart of Canada's oldest black settlement. With a museum, an auditorium, a reference library, photographic exhibits, a research and publications program and public education services, the Black Cultural Centre for Nova Scotia is a monument to the black presence and contribution.

Other notable black secular organizations in Nova Scotia are the George Washington Carver Credit Union (1950), the Black Business Consortium (1981), the North Preston Ratepayers Association (late 1940s), the Black Professional Women's Group (1969), the East Preston Lions Club (1977), the Afro-Canadian Caucus of Nova Scotia and the Nova Scotia Home for Coloured Children still active in 1993 after a long and distinguished existence since 1921. There are many other organizations throughout the province, notably community or church based.

For a Nova Scotian black population in 1993 of approximately 20,000 there is no shortage of issues, some historical and a few emerging contemporary ones. Of the historical issues, that of racism, unequal educational opportunities, chronic unemployment and under-employment continue to persist. On the contemporary scene, the emerging issues are the expectations of youth, increased emphasis on affirmative action programs to provide access to education, employment equity, diversity in employment and more active participation in politics.

In January, 1989, friction developed between white and black students at Cole Harbour District High School which led to a charge of racism in the Nova Scotia school system spearheaded by the Parent and Student Association of Preston. PSAP called repeatedly and unsuccessfully for a public inquiry into racism in the school system. This call has not disappeared in 1993 but the response to it now is an acknowledgment that indeed it does exist and something has to be done about it. The Halifax County-Bedford District School Board—the parent of Cole Harbour District High School—has responded positively in other ways: it held public hearings and formulated new policies to combat the various manifestations of racism in the total school environment. It appointed a Supervisor of Race Relations, Cross-Cultural Understanding and Human Rights. Other school boards have adopted similar policies or are in the process of doing so. In the meantime, the Black

Educators Association, the Black Learners Advisory Committee, the Nova Scotia Department of Education, as well as institutions of higher learning are all cooperating for positive changes. Surely, the result of all these efforts from various quarters will produce the desired results before the twentieth century comes to an end?

The events at Cole Harbour District High School attracted attention all over Canada and even beyond. The media portrayed it as race riots of tremendous proportions; organizations and institutions all over Canada invited resource persons from Nova Scotia to speak about these events and their implications for race relations. Indeed the present writer was one such person invited to present a paper on the subject at a conference in Toronto on strategies for alternative dispute resolution.

As Cole Harbour began to fade into the background of public consciousness in Nova Scotia, another set of events in July, 1991 put the spotlight back on Nova Scotia, on racism and race relations. The events began on July 19, 1991 with a disturbance at a downtown Halifax night club, an incident which was seen as resulting from the longstanding frustrations of the black community stemming from systemic discrimination in education, employment, housing and services.

The response was immediate: numerous meetings were held involving individuals and representatives of black organizations and all levels of government; a peace march symbolizing the quest for racial harmony was spearheaded by the Reverend Darryl Gray and the Nova Scotia Cultural Awareness Youth Group; an Advisory Group on Race Relations was set up with representatives from the three levels of government and the black community. The chairperson of the Advisory Group is Carolyn Thomas, a prominent Nova Scotian Black and Coordinator of Affirmative Action of the Nova Scotia Human Rights Commission. Other members drawn from the black community were: Archy Beals, Ken Hudson, Alma Johnston, Allister Johnson, Janis Jones-Darrell, Reverend Oqueri Ohanaka, Dolly Williams and Cecil Wright.

On September 1, 1991, the Advisory Group came up with 94 recommendations touching upon all areas that influenced and affected the condition of Blacks in Nova Scotia: education, employment and economic development, black community participation and access to services, policing, justice and human rights, black community development, communications and the media and tourism and culture.

This remarkable document is a blueprint for black advancement in Nova Scotia and a model much sought after in other parts of the country.

Carolyn Thomas.

The Nova Scotia government responded to the 94 recommendations on October 15, 1991 through the Honourable Joel R. Matheson, Q.C., Minister responsible for the Administration of the Nova Scotia Human Rights Act, whose introduction included the following statement:

"The government of Nova Scotia intends that this response will set a tone and spirit of inclusion for all minority groups in the province. It is clear that many of the Advisory group's recommendations deal with minority problems and concerns in general."

The government has agreed to provide periodic reports to show what progress continues to be made in implementing the 94 recommendations. There is no question that it will take many, many years to fully implement the 94 recommendations. The saving grace is that the diagnostic work is done; the recommendations are in place; they have all been accepted; changes are taking place gradually; a monitoring system is being put in place. The twenty-first century will judge race relations in Nova Scotia using the 94 recommendations of the Advisory Group as the measurement for success or failure.

Another yardstick will be the responses to the 81 recommendations contained in the Report of the Royal Commission on the Prosecution of Donald Marshall, Jr. which severely criticized both the justice system as well as race relations in Nova Scotia in January, 1990. One of the recommendations recalled here was that a Race Relations Division should be created in he Nova Scotia Human Rights Commission. This was implemented in 1991. The acting head of that Division in 1992-3 is Carolyn Thomas mentioned earlier as also the Chairperson of the Advisory Group on Race Relations.

Much has happened in Nova Scotia in the closing years of the twentieth century. A summary of new publications, new faces and new politics will be given in the concluding section of this chapter.

For the size of its black population, it is understandable that activities and organizations working on behalf of this sector in other parts of the Maritimes would be relatively fewer than in Nova Scotia. Population figures from Statistics Canada are not particularly helpful in identifying numbers. The following figures of 1986 are deemed to be generally on the low side:

	Blacks of single origin	Blacks of multiple origin
Newfoundland	55	125
Nova Scotia	7855	5060
New Brunswick	935	1145
Prince Edward Island	50	225

More reliable figures are promised for the 1991 census due to be released later in 1993.

One feature of black history which has been a durable and tragic part of Maritime and Canadian history is that of racial discrimination—a blight that continues to plague the land in spite of all the continuing efforts to eradicate it. Prince Edward Island is no exception.

Examples are available: in the 1950s, Louis Armstrong and his band were refused accommodation in Charlottetown; in 1962, a black medical doctor and his family were refused accommodation in a North Shore summer hotel where we are informed "discrimination on the grounds of race is general . . . and extends not only to Negroes, but also to Jewish and French Canadian families."*

In a decade since the Prince Edward Island Human Rights Commission came into existence in 1976, of the 196 complaints received five related to racial discrimination. In Nova Scotia comparative figures would show that in the early 1990s of some 250 to 300 formal complaints in a single year on average, the three top grounds relate to gender, race and disability, with gender and race running almost even. Of the cases most difficult to investigate and to determine are those related to complaints of racial discrimination or discrimination based on grounds of colour, ethnicity and national origins. There are subtleties and systemic barriers that are hard and hidden and difficult to penetrate and bring out into the open to be weighed on the scales of justice. While "tolerance" is no longer the desirable end to centuries-old racial injustices, the road ahead for unqualified acceptance of fellow human beings remains full of challenges. The author of Bla*ck islanders* presents the case in commendable choice of words:

"Over the years Island society has become more racially tolerant. But lingering stereotypes of Blacks, reinforced by North American mass media, still lead to some incongruous behaviour. A middle-aged professional man of West Indian origin has been addressed as though he were an African student. He has also noticed with mixed amusement and concern that some women who see him behind them in a store aisle will instinctively clutch their purses in front of them. And once when his son was doing odd jobs, his employer wondered if the boy's mother would be available to clean his house.

The next question, of course, is whether tolerance is enough. Just as freedom from slavery did not create equality, neither does tolerance. Tolerance alone is a fragile thread of stability which leaves the threat of racism suspended over the heads of those who are vulnerable."†

In a telephone interview with David Peters, vice-president of PRUDE in New Brunswick on January 19, 1993, this black resident of Saint John likened that city to the "diamond of Canada" but elaborated thus:

"Prejudice is so polished in this city that it is like a diamond."

* Jim Hornby, *Black Islanders*, p. 100
† Jim Hornby, *Black Islanders*, p. 101.

PRUDE—whose origins are mentioned in an earlier chapter—continues to be actively led by its president of many years, Carl A. White, Jr. As part of its growth since 1981, PRUDE additionally sponsors Black Employment Counselling, the Immigrant Settlement and Adaptation Program, the Settlement Language Training Program and the HOST program—the last-named matches people from the Saint John community with government-sponsored refugees who have settled in the Saint John area.

The responsibility for coordinating the many activities of PRUDE rests with its Coordinator, Teala Cain, who has held this office since 1988 and represents PRUDE on other organization and agencies, besides serving as speaker and panelist at conferences and symposia.

The accomplishments of PRUDE are all the more remarkable since it does as a single organization what Nova Scotia is fortunate to have done through separate specialist organizations. In this regard, the vice-president of PRUDE has served the organization, the community, the city of Saint John and the province of New Brunswick well. As education consultant, television host, black historian and producer of Black History Kit, David Peters has traversed the city and the province speaking to students and community groups about black history, culture, contributions and accomplishments.

Through such efforts PRUDE has participated in an exhibition on African Art at the Aitken Bicentennial Centre and the Africville exhibition at the New Brunswick Museum in Saint John from January 10, 1993 to the end of February, 1993 when the exhibition returned to Nova Scotia to be housed in its permanent location, the Black Cultural Centre for Nova Scotia.

For as long as the pioneering and persevering work of PRUDE continues, black history and culture in the Maritimes will be well served. Little known facts will then surface and the total Canadian society will be the beneficiary. One example is the research on the profiles of six New Brunswick women to mark International Women's Day, 1992, which resulted in a place for Anna Minerva Henderson reported to be the first black female civil servant in the early twentieth century in Canada.

PRUDE was awarded the Peace Medal for its role in the local community of Saint John in December, 1992. Accepting the award, Carl A. White, Jr., spoke for more than PRUDE or Saint John or New Brunswick:

"In order for us to exist in harmony and peace, we must realize we are all somebody—we are all equal."

II. The Road to the 21st Century

In 1993, seven years remain to the 21st century. Already new faces, new publications, new politics and new prospects bode well for the coming century. There will be no *end* to the philosophies and practices of discriminatory social and human behaviour, but every generation will raise its standards of what it deems to be acceptable human behaviour and will define its prescriptions and penalties for what it deems to be unacceptable human behaviour.

The new black actors on the scene have already emerged and many more are lining up in classrooms, universities, workplaces and political organizations. The new deacons, licentiates, program directors, civil servants, professionals, politicians, entrepreneurs, teachers, administrators and community activists have the opportunity and the responsibility to firstly set the standards for themselves and secondly the standards for others.

One black American writer, Dr. Shelby Steele, has grappled with the issues of race, power and morality in a book published in 1990 entitled: *A New Vision of Race in America. The Content of Our Character.* In it he tries to explain what made the late Dr. Martin Luther King, Jr. the great leader he was:

"King understood that racial power subverts moral power, and he pushed the principles of fairness and equality rather than black power because he believed those principles would bring Blacks their most complete liberation. He sacrificed race for morality and his innocence was made genuine by that sacrifice. What made King the most powerful and extraordinary black leader of this century was not his race but his morality."*

Choices are being made and have to continue to be made. Many success stories are surfacing. Take Barbara Ann Hamilton of Beechville, a predominantly black community on the outskirts of Halifax, Nova Scotia. This remarkable young person graduated in 1991 with a B.A. degree in recreation administration and has already served on the boards of many organizations. As a youth worker with the City of Halifax recreation department, Barbara Hamilton is putting her philosophies into practice:

"Now she's helping kids from lower income families, black and white, realize they can accomplish what they want

* Page 19.

Sylvia Hamilton.

Black Cultural Centre

because of who they are, not what others think."*

* *Mail Star*, July 24, 1992.

An emerging educational strategist calling upon African-Nova Scotians to embrace a unified educational agenda is Dr. Harvey H. Millar, member of the faculty of commerce at Saint Mary's University and a founding member of the African-Canadian Education Project. Citing the numerous educational programs and strategies aimed at addressing the impact of racism, Dr. Millar argues that:

"Unfortunately, all the . . . programs did not emerge under a unified educational agenda defined by African-Nova Scotians. They emerged, for the most part, from knee-jerk reactions to pressure from the African-Nova Scotian community . . . ."

Dr. Millar's point is that for an education strategy and agenda to succeed two needs have to be served: the individual need and the community need.

The debates continue at various levels and in different forms producing results on various fronts: two black Nova Scotians, Walter Borden and George Boyd have put the black talent and voice to excellent use on the stage, radio and television. Mention was made of Walter Borden in an earlier chapter. Thirty-eight year old George Boyd, co-anchor of CBC Newsworld in Halifax, is the moving spirit behind the formation of a Canadian Black Theatre Group. Writer of the excellent play, *Shine Boy*, a musical biography of Halifax-born famous black boxer, George Dixon, George Boyd is a presence and a voice that transcends boundaries.

The work of Sylvia Hamilton in film production is a significant contribution by another black Nova Scotian. Co-producer of "Black Mother Black Daughter" in 1990, Sylvia Hamilton has come through once again with a second production entitled "Speak It! From the Heart of Black Nova Scotia". The premiere screening was held at Saint Patrick's High School, Halifax, on February 5, 1993.

The appearance of new publications by young Nova Scotian black writers is nothing less than an intellectual revolution: Maxine Tynes, *Borrowed Beauty*, David Woods *Native Song*, George Elliot Clarke, *Fire on the Water, Saltwater Spirituals and Deeper Blues* and *Wylah Falls* and Charles Saunders, *Sweat and Soul*. The work of Henry Bishop, Curator at the Black Cultural Centre enriches the production of writers and artists. Born in Weymouth Falls in 1952, he is a graduate of the Nova Scotia College of Art and Design. His numerous logos exemplify black history and culture.

No other period in the history of black Maritimers has seen such

Maxine Tynes.

Black Cultural Centre

literary output in the space of a few years by such an array of talented young writers. The challenge now is to other sectors to do as well.

Rose Jarvis, George Elliott Clarke and Fran McNeil, President Weymouth Historical Society.

One such testing ground is the political arena. Blacks in Nova Scotia have participated in municipal politics for many decades. Thomas Johnson was elected councillor in Halifax County in 1903. Over the years many black councillors followed in his footsteps. Councillor Wayne Adams, the incumbent in 1993, was first elected in 1979. In the city of Halifax, Graham Downey was first elected in 1971 and is still serving in 1993. In Amherst, Councillor Donald Paris was first elected in 1971 and is still in office. Councillor Daurene Lewis was elected at Annapolis Royal in 1979 and became mayor in 1984—the first black mayor in all of Canada. In Sydney, Nova Scotia, Thomas E. Miller was elected in 1955 and served for 17 years and Eddie Paris served from 1975 to 1988.

Donald H. Oliver, Q.C. of Halifax was appointed to the Senate in October 1990.

The Nova Scotia provincial elections held on May 25, 1993 pro-

Henry Bishop, visual artist/designer, curator, Black Cultural Centre.

vided one feature of particular significance in the province's political history: the contest for the newly created seat of Preston. This constitu-

The Honourable Wayne Adams (back row, 3rd from right), Minister of Supply and Services photographed with the Premier of Nova Scotia, The Honourable Dr. John Savage and Cabinet colleagues on June 11, 1993.

Government Information Services photo

ency comprised nearly 40 percent black voters and, of the four candidates who stood for election, three were Black: Wayne Adams (Liberal Party), Yvonne Atwell (New Democratic Party) and Darryl Gray (Progressive Conservative Party). The fourth candidate was David Hendsbee (Independent). Adams won with 36 percent of the vote while Hendsbee was runner-up with 29 percent.

A columnist Charles Saunders put it, "History has been made, and Wayne Adams deserves full credit for making it the right way.*

There was more history-making to follow when Wayne Adams was appointed the first Black Cabinet minister in the province's history on June 11, 1993. "The new minister has had a history of making history since the 1960s, when he became the province's first black radio announcer and hosted Black Journal, a radical show for its day."†

This political development is one further indication that the closing

* *The Sunday Daily News*, May 30, 1993.
† Janice Tibbetts, writing in *The Mail Star*, June 12, 1993.

years of the twentieth century have seen the placemat of achievement and black aspirations higher on the province's landscape. With this heightened position, comes increased responsibilities which the Honourable Wayne Adams, Minister of Supply and Services, acknowledges:

"My role is to reflect an image of my people so that we can change attitudes."*

The challenges are daunting but the directions are clear. With seven years to go to the 21st century, black Maritimers as well as other Maritimers can all expect to face difficult times and difficult choices. The days of plenty and prosperity will fade with the 20th century. Educational standards will rise, job competition will be fierce. Charles Darwin's theory of "survival of the fittest" may assume frightening proportions for the lesser prepared. Demographic realities are expected to change dramatically and this will surely place historical agendas and priorities in a collision course with contemporary agendas and priorities.

In order to overcome odds and to be equipped to meet the challenges of the 21st century, black youth should pay serious attention to the advice of fellow black youth, Barbara Ann Hamilton:

"When they (youth) have a problem, I tell them it's not easy, but once you get your education, no one can take it away from you . . . Education opens doors."†

One can echo the words of black Nova Scotian, Barb Hamilton, that "it's not easy". It never was easy; it will never be easy. The dividing lines are formidable, but they must be crossed:

"At the heart of the fractured soul of America is the frightening chasm of race. So long as whites prefer to live in a world of dangerous illusions, while cynical politicians . . . peddle the poison of 'reverse discrimination', no genuine interracial dialogue is possible. Fighting for full equality, strong enforcement of affirmative action and challenging the myths about race are the only steps which will achieve real understanding across the colour line."**

To be able to carry out this fight for equality, for affirmative action, for demystifying notions of superiority, one will need the mental fortitude that comes from sound education.

* Ibid
† *The Mail Star*, July 24, 1992.
** Dr. Manning Marable, "Along the Colour Line", *The Spectrum*, April 15, 1992.

Select Bibliography

Best, Carrie M. *That Lonesome Road*, New Glasgow, 1977.

Boyd, Frank, Stanley. Ed., *McKerrow, A Brief History of Blacks in Nova Scotia, 1783-1895*, Dartmouth, 1975.

Campbell, Douglas F. *Banked Fires: The Ethnics of Nova Scotia*, Ontario, 1978.

Clarke, George Elliott, Ed., *Fire on the Water. An Anthology of Black Nova Scotian Writing*, Vols. I and II, Lawrencetown, Nova Scotia, 1992.

Clarke, George Elliott (Ed.,) *Fire on the Water*, Vols. I and II, Lawrencetown, NS, 1992.

Clairmont, Donald H. and Magill, Dennis W. *Africville: The Life and Death of a Canadian Black Community*, Toronto, 1974.

Clairmont, Donald H. and Magill, Dennis W. *Nova Scotian Blacks: An Historical and Structural Overview*, Halifax, 1970.

Don Clairmont, Stephen Kimber, Bridglal Pachai and Charles Saunders, *The Spirit of Africville*, Halifax, 1992.

D'Oyley, Vincent. *Black Presence in Multi-Ethnic Canada*, Toronto, 1978.

Fergusson, C.B. *A Documentary Study of the Negroes in Nova Scotia Between the War of 1812 and the Winning of Responsible Government*, Halifax 1948.

Gordon, Grant, *From Slavery to Freedom. The Life of David George, Pioneer Black Baptist Minister*, Wolfville and Hantsport, Nova Scotia, 1992.

Grant, John N. "Black Immigrants into Nova Scotia", *Journal of Negro History*, Vol. 58, No. 3, July 1973.

Grant, John N. *Black Nova Scotians*, Halifax, 1980.

Grant, John N. "The 1821 Emigration of Black Nova Scotians to Trinidad", Vol. 2, No. 3, September 1972.

Grant, John N. "The Immigration and Settlement of the Black Refugees of the War of 1812 in Nova Scotia and New Brunswick", M.A. thesis, U.N.B., May 1970.

Grant, John N. *The Immigration and Settlement of the Black Refugees*, Westphal, Nova Scotia, 1990. Revised with fresh illustrations.

Hornby, Jim *Black Islanders. Prince Edward Island's Historical Black Community*, Charlottetown, 1991.

Oliver, Pearleen. *A Brief History of the Coloured Baptists of Nova Scotia, 1782-1953*, Halifax, 1954.

Pachai, Bridglal Ed., *Canadian Black Studies*, Halifax, 1979.

Pachai, Bridglal. *Beneath the Clouds of the Promised Land. Survival of Nova Scotia's Blacks, Vol. I, 1600-1800,* Halifax, 1987.

Pachai, Bridglal. —-*Vol. II, 1800-1989*, Halifax, 1991.

Ruck, Calvin W. *Canada's Black Battalion. No. 2 Construction 1916 - 1920*, Westphal, 1986 and Halifax, 1987.

Saunders, Charles R. *Sweat and Soul. The Saga of Black Boxers From the Halifax Forum to Caesar's Palace*, Westphal and Hantsport, Nova Scotia, 1990.

Spray, W.A. *The Blacks in New Brunswick*, Fredericton, 1972.

Walker, James W. St. G. *A History of Blacks in Canada. A Study Guide for Teachers and Students*, 1980 (contains comprehensive book titles).

Walker, James W. St. G. *The Black Loyalists. The Search for a Promised Land in Nova Scotia and Sierra Leone*, New York, 1976.

Wilson, Ellen Gibson. *The Loyal Blacks*, Toronto, 1976.

Winks, Robin W. *The Blacks in Canada*, Montreal, 1971 (contains comprehensive book titles).

Various journal articles consulted have not been listed. These appear in the valuable bibliographies available in the works of Robin Winks and James Walker, listed above.